Disclaimer
This workbook is intended to provide helpful and informative material on the subjects addressed. The reader should consult a personal health and mental health professional before adopting any of these suggestions in this book or drawing inferences from it. The author expressly disclaims responsibility for any adverse effects arising from the user application of the information.

*If you or someone you know is having thoughts of self-harm, suicide, or harm to others, immediately call 911.

Table of Contents

Note From the Author   1

About the Authors   2

Intro   4

How To Use This Journal   7

Primary Emotions List   13

The Six Basic Emotions   15

Unhelpful Thinking Styles   16

Let's Begin   19

Sample Guide To Resolve Your Emotion   20

My Emotions Journal Pages   21

Emotions and Feelings Glossary   141

Note From the Author

Thank you for picking up this journal. I have spent the last 14 years helping people bring helpful resolutions to their emotions. It was quickly evident that a self-guided journal would be helpful. So, I have infused tools, tips, and a simplified process for your journal within this book to help you think about your emotions differently. I will guide you to help you ask the right questions about what your emotions tell you and discover the answers your emotions need. I really hope you can use the My Emotions Journal as a guide as often as needed.

As always, you can check out more comprehensive resources, including some guided courses I have available if you want to learn more about your emotions.

Dr. Ally Butrous
Author, Life Coach, Nutrition Coach
DrAllyButrous.com

About Dr. Authors

 DR. ALLY is a Life Coach, Author, and Podcaster. She specializes in helping high-achievers and ambitious individuals reach their goals and peak performance, reduce stress, and gain emotional intelligence, clarity, confidence, and empowering self-talk! Her work has been featured in blogs, bestselling books, TV, and YouTube Channels. Her favorite hobby is traveling. She and her husband, Jeremy, have been to 68 countries so far!

Dr. Ally knows what it takes to perform at high levels. She graduated High School 4 years early by passing the California High School Proficiency Exam and started college just after she turned 15. By 16, she was a nationally ranked All American college athlete. Despite those achievements, she had many unhelpful mindsets, and terrible self-talk and confidence. Her outward achievements were not enough to make her feel like she was happy or thriving.

She began reading self-help books and listening to self-help programs, which she credits with changing her life. She soon developed a very systematic way of applying self-help principles and information to her life. This led her to a deep sense of compassion for those similarly struggling. She decided to study psychology, and she focused her doctoral research on positive psychology. She is now passionate about helping others have concrete tools, systems and roadmaps to develop their best life.

Choosing to forgo the path of becoming a licensed psychologist, therapist, or treating mental illness, she instead focuses her work on helping high achievers custom build their ideal life, and remove any barriers to their success.

JEREMY BUTROUS lives in Los Angeles with his wife, Dr. Ally. He has written over 30 books, some of which are ghostwritten. He loves to see people reach their full potential and purpose in life. He is a content strategist. Jeremy's most recent book is Learning How to Love with Dr. Ally.

Intro

Every human has emotions. In the past, there has been an idea that the only people who need to spend time working with and understanding their emotions are significantly struggling to manage their emotions, or dealing with a mental health diagnosis. In fact, that is as silly as saying the only person who needs to spend time working out or taking care of their body is the person whose body is struggling or dealing with a health diagnosis.

That is not the case at all! Those of us who want a thriving body and thriving emotions are proactive and learn all we can to have an advantage! Emotional intelligence and management are vital to helping us all achieve our goals. They can help us create more positive work days, have more emotional energy, feel happier, have better relationships, and feel more fulfilled.

The goal of this journal is to help us process emotions to come to a solution that will ultimately serve us, our goals, our community, and society in a positive way. It is essential to note that our emotions do not give us information regarding others. They are not gossipers; they are only feedback to us. In the same way, a car's dashboard doesn't tell you anything about any car other than that car. Blaming others for our emotions will not help us resolve them.

A big point of confusion when it comes to resolving emotion is that we often confuse an emotion with an action. This makes it harder to accept the helpfulness of all emotions and explore what they are saying. For example, an emotion of anger is helpful in accepting, processing, and understanding. An action of anger is not helpful. Screaming at your boss (or yourself) or hurting yourself or others in any way does not resolve anger at all.

An action made in anger is just a physical manifestation of unprocessed anger. Acting in anger does not teach you what you need to set yourself up for less anger in the future. The same is true for happiness. Acting out of happiness (smiling, dancing around, etc) does not teach you why you are happy or what you need to do to increase your happiness overall. You have to process what happiness is teaching you in order to take action to create more happiness in your life intentionally. That is the goal of this journal.

Your emotions are JUST messages. Emotions are not good, bad, right, or wrong. Say that with me over and over until that sinks in. Emotions are not good or bad; they are JUST messages. So many believe that we have good and bad emotions, and therefore, they deny having the "bad emotions," or they bury them deep and pretend they are no longer there. This mentality causes people to go numb or explode because they are not providing a reasonable answer for the message their emotion is presenting.

In order to have confidence in and with our emotions, we have to start appreciating and accepting them for what they actually are! A tooth doesn't ache because it's being dramatic or difficult. A tooth just tells you information so you can make changes before you have a much worse problem! It also motivates you to learn hygiene tools and skills to prevent it from hurting in the future. The same is true about our emotions.

If we feel sad or stressed, our emotions are informing us about something so we can make changes! If we have been taught to ignore our "negative" emotions, the messages build up, like plaque, and make things worse! Regular emotional hygiene and checkups can keep us Healthy!

Emotions are like our phones, giving us messages. But if we keep getting notification after notification and don't resolve them, they continue to make noise and bug us! When we accept our emotions, get the message, and resolve it, our confidence grows, and we become free to choose what new emotion we would like to have.

Emotions are derived from one's instinctive state of mind from one's circumstances. They are life's excellent communicators. Don't hurt the messenger; find out what they are saying! We all have strong emotions speak to us loudly and incessantly and soft emotions that clothe us in peace. Emotions keep us plugged into ourselves and our environment and relationships. Emotions can be key indicators of health. Emotions are vital to who we are. They tell us when we should check in with ourselves when things are going well, and when things are off.

We have the power to change our emotions, produce new emotions, and respond to the emotions we feel. Be patient with yourself as you learn more about emotional intelligence. Just like any other skill, you can learn, grow, and get better at it.

How To Use This Journal

Every section in this journal is to help you learn, discover, process, and act on your emotions in positive ways.

List of Emotions

Every emotion we have needs to be self-identified. Expanding your understanding of what emotions are available helps you to understand the message, need, and action adequately. Also, you will have a more robust list of emotions that will help you communicate what you are feeling to others. I have provided you with an extensive list of emotions broken up into primary emotion categories. Please get to know this list, as it will be the language you use when identifying your emotions. The more emotions you know, the better you will identify the messages you are being told.

*Please use the Primary List of Emotions (located at the front of the Journal) and the Emotions and Feelings Glossary (Located at the back of the Journal)

Emotions Journal Entry

So you had an emotion! Congratulations! Some emotions are loud and powerful, and others are passive and calming. However, each emotion is telling us something. We can discover the meaning behind the emotion by asking ourselves helpful questions. The more honest we are, the better this process will be. After discovering the emotion and identifying what it is saying, we need to put together action steps to resolve the message. This will help us be emotionally healthy.

Below, you will see a sample My Emotions Entry. I have set up a way for you to follow the guided prompts to unpack your emotions. Ask yourself helpful questions along the way that bring you moments of reflection and resolution. Each My Emotions entry is set up to guide you through one emotion at a time. If you have more than one emotion, perhaps you need to complete another entry to answer the questions that emotion presents. You will get the hang of it after a bit of practice.

Where is your emotion coming from?

Are your Emotions from the distant past?
Inside the emotions journal entry, did you discover that your emotion was created in the distant past? You now have two areas to pursue self-discovery. First, you want to assess the emotion you are feeling today and, secondarily, the emotion that you first felt in your distant past. I recommend that you complete the present tense moment entry (the emotions you have now) and start a new entry for the past emotion (the moment in the past that you believe it started).

Our Bodies

Your body is a communication machine! If you are hungry, it will tell you; if you are not feeling good, it will tell you. That is how we were made. Sometimes, if our mood is off and we are producing all kinds of emotions, it's good to check in with your body and make sure it is getting what it needs. Did you have too much to eat? Are you sick? Did you get enough sleep? Are you drinking the right amount of water? Go through the same process in My Emotions Entry to identify the origin of your emotions and see what changes need to be made. Your emotions will be affected if you are experiencing physical symptoms of any kind. Be sure to get checked out by a doctor, get your blood labs done, and stay healthy to ensure you are giving your body everything it needs.

Unhelpful Thinking Styles

Emotions can come from unhelpful thinking styles. I have composed some common unhelpful thinking styles that can trigger us to have an emotion. You may discover more unhelpful thinking styles that are not on this list, and I encourage you to write them down. If you identify that your emotions came from an unhelpful thinking style, then complete the Resolve My Emotion entry and work on replacing your thoughts with helpful ones in the needs and action steps.

* Please see the list and examples in the identified section.

Emotions Messages and Emotions Actions

You will have the opportunity to work through many primary and secondary emotions within the Resolving My Emotions sections. You will see an entire two-page spread dedicated to the Emotional Messages. What is your emotion saying? What is it telling you? Where is it coming from? Once you have that information, you will see the next two-page spread dedicated to Emotional Actions. Now that you know where your emotion came from and what it is saying, you can put actions together. What should you do with the message you have received? Should you deploy different boundaries, treat yourself differently, or change your environment? The plan of action should be specific to the emotion and its messages.

The first 30 journal pages will help you think proactively about situations when you felt the specific emotion labeled for you. Each of the 15 emotions have two opportunities to explore how you might resolve them. The thought bubbles contain ideas and inspiration first for what the emotion could mean, then how to resolve it. This gives you proactive practice to gain confidence. The next 30 pages give you space to explore what an emotion is teaching you in the moment you feel it, so the emotion space is left blank for you to fill.

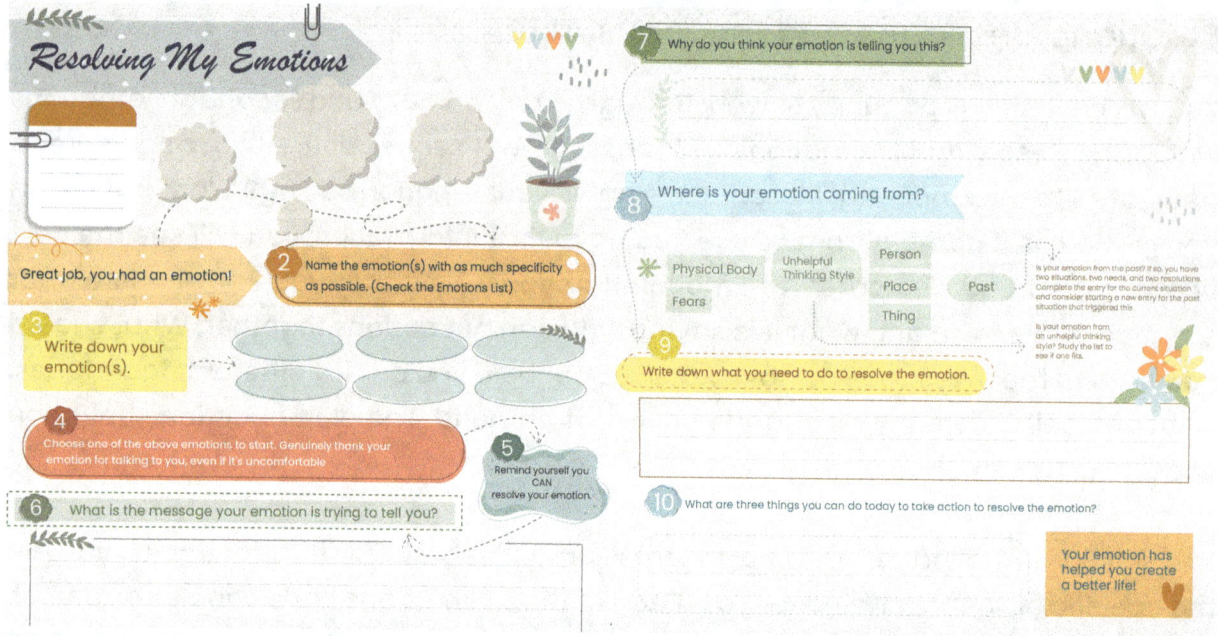

Resolving My Emotions

Great job, you had an emotion!

2. Name the emotion(s) with as much specificity as possible. (Check the Emotions List)

3. Write down your emotion(s).

4. Choose one of the above emotions to start. Genuinely thank your emotion for talking to you, even if it's uncomfortable

5. Remind yourself you CAN resolve your emotion.

6. What is the message your emotion is trying to tell you?

7. Why do you think your emotion is telling you this?

8. Where is your emotion coming from?

Physical Body   Unhelpful Thinking Style   Person   Place   Past   Thing

Fears

Is your emotion from the past? If so, you have two situations, two needs, and two resolutions. Complete the entry for the current situation and consider starting a new entry for the past situation that triggered this.

Is your emotion from an unhelpful thinking style? Study the list to see if one fits.

9. Write down what you need to do to resolve the emotion.

10. What are three things you can do today to take action to resolve the emotion?

Your emotion has helped you create a better life!

Below is the question and answer sequence you will find in the emotional message and emotional action journal pages.

1. Great job, you had an emotion!
2. Name the emotion(s) with as much specificity as possible
3. Write down your emotion(s)
4. Validate your emotions. Genuinely thank your emotions for talking to you, even if it's uncomfortable.
5. Remind yourself you CAN resolve your emotions.
6. What message is your emotion trying to tell you?
7. Why do you think your emotions are telling you this?

8. Is your emotion coming from your past, fears, unhelpful thinking styles, environment, or physical body (e.g., hunger, exhaustion)?
9. Write down what you need to do to move forward and fulfill the emotion. Take action to meet the need.
10. What are three things you can do today to take action to resolve the emotion?

Congratulations, you have created positive options to fulfill your emotions!

Emotion = Meaning = Need = Action

Each emotion should be identified, and meaning should be placed on what it is saying. Ask yourself what needs should be assigned and what action should be taken. You can have the same emotion daily and have a new meaning, need, and action. So, be mindful of the changes each and every time.

Primary List of Emotions

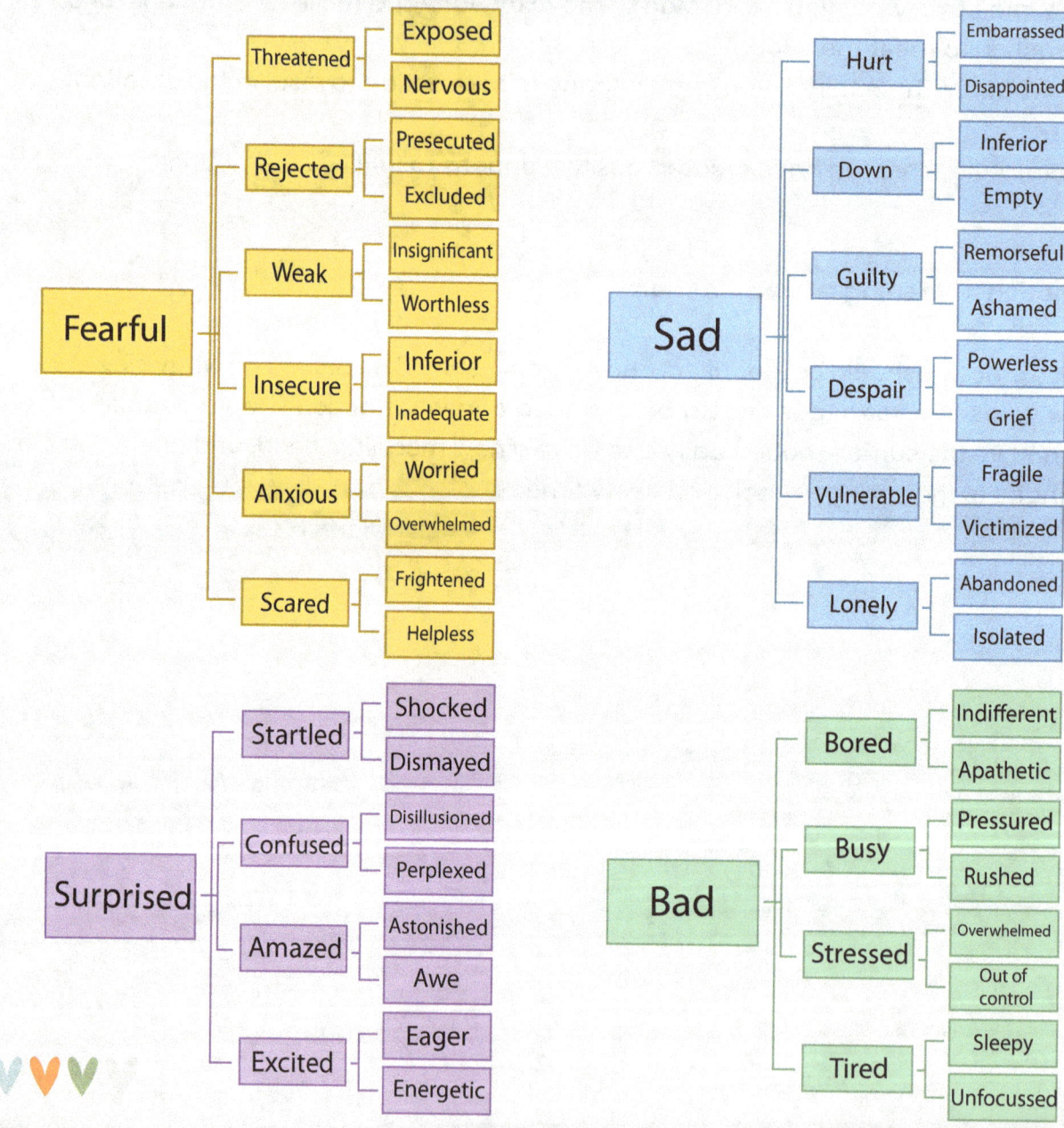

Fearful
- Threatened
  - Exposed
  - Nervous
- Rejected
  - Presecuted
  - Excluded
- Weak
  - Insignificant
  - Worthless
- Insecure
  - Inferior
  - Inadequate
- Anxious
  - Worried
  - Overwhelmed
- Scared
  - Frightened
  - Helpless

Sad
- Hurt
  - Embarrassed
  - Disappointed
- Down
  - Inferior
  - Empty
- Guilty
  - Remorseful
  - Ashamed
- Despair
  - Powerless
  - Grief
- Vulnerable
  - Fragile
  - Victimized
- Lonely
  - Abandoned
  - Isolated

Surprised
- Startled
  - Shocked
  - Dismayed
- Confused
  - Disillusioned
  - Perplexed
- Amazed
  - Astonished
  - Awe
- Excited
  - Eager
  - Energetic

Bad
- Bored
  - Indifferent
  - Apathetic
- Busy
  - Pressured
  - Rushed
- Stressed
  - Overwhelmed
  - Out of control
- Tired
  - Sleepy
  - Unfocussed

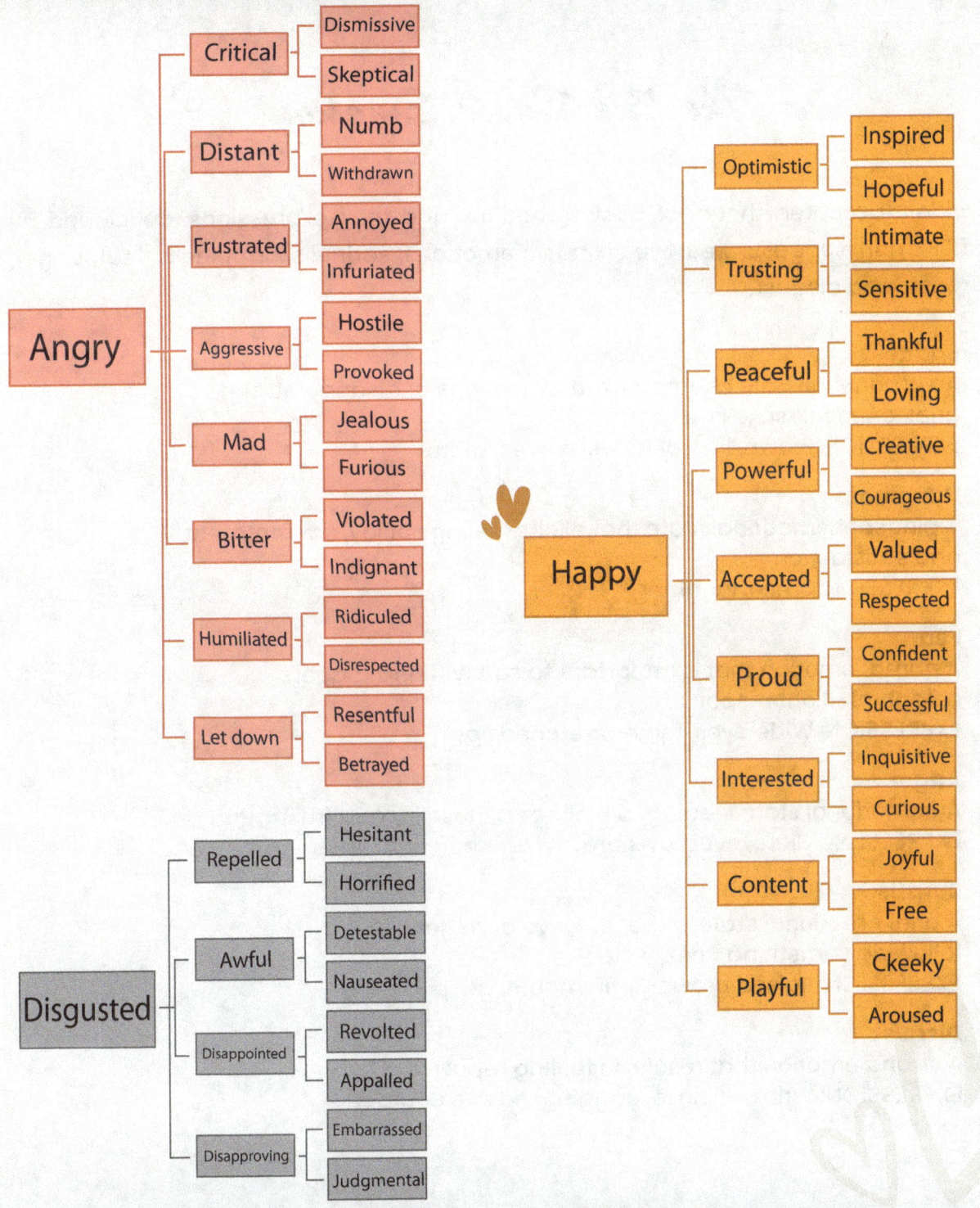

Angry
- Critical
  - Dismissive
  - Skeptical
- Distant
  - Numb
  - Withdrawn
- Frustrated
  - Annoyed
  - Infuriated
- Aggressive
  - Hostile
  - Provoked
- Mad
  - Jealous
  - Furious
- Bitter
  - Violated
  - Indignant
- Humiliated
  - Ridiculed
  - Disrespected
- Let down
  - Resentful
  - Betrayed

Disgusted
- Repelled
  - Hesitant
  - Horrified
- Awful
  - Detestable
  - Nauseated
- Disappointed
  - Revolted
  - Appalled
- Disapproving
  - Embarrassed
  - Judgmental

Happy
- Optimistic
  - Inspired
  - Hopeful
- Trusting
  - Intimate
  - Sensitive
- Peaceful
  - Thankful
  - Loving
- Powerful
  - Creative
  - Courageous
- Accepted
  - Valued
  - Respected
- Proud
  - Confident
  - Successful
- Interested
  - Inquisitive
  - Curious
- Content
  - Joyful
  - Free
- Playful
  - Ckeeky
  - Aroused

The Six Basic Emotions

A widely accepted theory of basic emotions and their expressions, developed by Paul Ekman, suggests we have six basic emotions: sadness, happiness, fear, anger, surprise, and disgust.

1. **Sadness**
   An emotional state characterized by feelings of disappointment, grief, or hopelessness
   EXPRESSION: Frown, loss of focus in eyes, tears

2. **Happiness**
   A pleasant emotional state that elicits feelings of joy, contentment, and satisfaction
   EXPRESSION: Smile, laughter

3. **Fear**
   A primal emotion that is important to survival and triggers a fight-or-flight response
   EXPRESSION: Wide eyes, tense stretched lips

4. **Anger**
   An emotional state leading to feelings of hostility and frustration
   EXPRESSION: Glare, eyebrows drawn together, tight lips

5. **Surprise**
   A brief emotional state, either positive or negative, following something unexpected
   EXPRESSION: Raised brows, open mouth, gasp

6. **Disgust**
   A strong emotion that results in feeling repulsed
   EXPRESSION: Wrinkled nose, gagging, no eye contact

Unhelpful Thinking Styles

Below are kinds of thinking that drain our energy, vitality, power, productivity, and happiness. By finding an alternative way to think, we will decrease uncomfortable emotional experiences and likely be more successful in many domains.

ALL-OR-NOTHING	Using language that divides things into either-or options, or perfectionistic standards.
SUPERVILLAN	Trying to read minds, or predict the future. And usually you predict it's all bad!
DICTATOR	Using demanding, judgmental, shaming non-negotiable words. Creating arbitrary standards we hold ourselves to. Blaming and labeling. Using the words, "always" or "never." "Everyone," "no one," and "can't".
HORROR FILM	Phrases that include idioms, or add intensity, but do not accurately describe the situation. Because of that, it can never be resolved.
SCARCITY	Thinking in a way that assumes resources, opportunities, people, or abilities are limited.
OVERSIMPLIFIED	Trying to make sense of a situation by ignoring the complexity and focusing on just one part of the situation.

Unhelpful Thinking Examples

Here are examples of what unhelpful thinking actually sounds like in our thoughts.

ALL-OR-NOTHING	If I make one mistake, I have failed. I won't try it if I am not already good at it.
SUPERVILLAN	They must think I am an idiot! I know the future will not be better.
DICTATOR	I don't deserve better. I will never be good enough. I am broken, I am bad. It's all my fault. I will always be sad. I will never make it. I can't do this.
HORROR FILM	I shot myself in the foot. They stabbed me in the back. Just kick me while I am down. They ran me over. It went down in flames.
SCARCITY	No one can help me. I will never have enough love, money, talent, clients, etc. That was my only way/ chance to _____.
OVERSIMPLIFIED	They are just being nice because they want something from me. If it wasn't for my boss, I'd be able to be happy.

Helpful Alternatives to unhelpful thinking

Below are alternative thoughts based on the examples on the previous page.

ALL-OR-NOTHING	One mistake doesn't sum up who I am. Trying and practicing is likely to improve how well I do something.
SUPERVILLAN	I can't read minds. If they are thinking something, it's their job to say it. I don't know what will happen in the future. I can only truly work with what I know in this moment.
DICTATOR	I don't deserve any better or worse than other humans. Who says what "good enough" is? I am not broken, I am human. How can I make it better instead of just calling myself names? I can put in more effort this week.
HORROR FILM	What do I really mean when I say this? What is a more helpful way to describe the situation to create a real life solution?
SCARCITY	Whatever is meant for me will find me, I may have made assumptions about how my needs would be met. There are other ways.
OVERSIMPLIFIED	They are likely being nice for many different reasons. I can work to have better boundaries with my boss, but I am in charge of working towards things that give me the feedback of happiness.

Let's Begin

Here are a few tips to help you as you begin journaling and resolving your emotions.

This is a process of guided self-discovery. It is simple and involves questions that will help you identify, listen, process, and take action steps to fulfill your emotions' beckoning. Think about these framing questions as you begin each journaling time until you get the hang of it.

Use "I feel" statements.

- What is it telling me to do? Why?
- Why is my mind and body telling me this?
- Is my feeling appropriate to the situation?
- Does your emotion match the expression assigned?
- What about the emotion is good? All emotions are beneficial; you are not allowed to say they are not.
- When did the emotion start? Why?
- What do you think that says about you?

1. Identify
2. Listen
3. Look at where it starts (ask really helpful questions)
4. Self-process (self-discovery)
5. Look at the next steps and actions to resolve each emotion

Sample Guide To Resolve Your Emotion

Emotions motivate us towards our best life. Below is an example of resolving emotions. These are not "right" or "wrong". They are just examples of how to use the tool.

There are hundreds of meanings, needs and actions for each and every emotion, so don't limit yourself to anything below. These are just a starting point.

EMOTION	MEANING	NEED	ACTION(S)
Sadness	I have lost or am missing something I value in life.	To notice the value and meaning it brought me. Healing.	Talk with a friend. Pursue values. Comfort myself.
Anger	My boundaries were crossed. I am feeling disrespected. I am being attacked.	Respect to be restored. Increased self-respect. Making changes to stop the same situation in the future.	Communicate and enforce boundaries.
Happiness	I am doing something that aligns with my values and is meaningful to me.	To continue to engage in these types of experiences.	Plan more of those kinds of activities.
Love	I am attached, or bonding with this person or activity. I respect and value it.	Invest time, energy, value, support, time and care.	Demonstrate my value, protect it.
Insecure	I do not know as much or have as much practice with something as I would like.	Accept I am still learning and practicing. Identify skills and ways to improve.	Make a plan to learn and practice.
Fear	Slow down, reassess the situation, pay attention.	To determine if the fear is coming from others, or my own thoughts.	Protect myself or change my thoughts.
Lonely	To connect with others or myself in a meaningful way.	To put effort into building relationships. To slop alienating myself.	Make a plan to increase social time.

Resolving My Emotions

Emotions Messages

Anger

What could anger be telling you?

> You are being motivated to set boundaries.

> Your expectations were not met.

> You have unhelpful assumptions that need to change.

Great job, you had an emotion!

2 Name the emotion(s) with as much specificity as possible. (Check the Emotions List)

3 Write down your emotion(s).

4 Choose one of the above emotions to start. Genuinely thank your emotion for talking to you, even if it's uncomfortable.

5 Remind yourself yo CAN resolve your emotio

6 What is the message your emotion is trying to tell you?

Why do you think your emotion is telling you this?

Where is your emotion coming from?

Physical Body

Unhelpful Thinking Style

Person

Place

Thing

Past

Fears

Is your emotion from the past? If so, you have two situations, two needs, and two resolutions. Complete the entry for the current situation and consider starting a new entry for the past situation that triggered this.

Is your emotion from an unhelpful thinking style? Study the list to see if one fits.

9 Write down what you need to do to resolve the emotion.

10 What are three things you can do today to take action to resolve the emotion?

Your emotion has helped you create a better life!

Resolving My Emotions

Emotions Action

Anger

Examples of actions that resolve anger.

Clarify and set boundaries.

Expressing your expectations or accepting the expectations is not realistic.

Focus on the facts, not assumptions.

Great job, you had an emotion!

2 Name the emotion(s) with as much specificity as possible. (Check the Emotions List)

3 Write down your emotion(s).

4 Choose one of the above emotions to start. Genuinely thank your emotion for talking to you, even if it's uncomfortable.

5 Remind yourself y CAN resolve your emoti

6 What is the message your emotion is trying to tell you?

Why do you think your emotion is telling you this?

Where is your emotion coming from?

Physical Body

Fears

Unhelpful Thinking Style

Person

Place

Thing

Past

Is your emotion from the past? If so, you have two situations, two needs, and two resolutions. Complete the entry for the current situation and consider starting a new entry for the past situation that triggered this.

Is your emotion from an unhelpful thinking style? Study the list to see if one fits.

9 Write down what you need to do to resolve the emotion.

10 What are three things you can do today to take action to resolve the emotion?

Your emotion has helped you create a better life!

Resolving My Emotions

Emotions Messages

Empowered

What could empower be telling you?

You took action and succeeded.

You have a helpful mindset.

You gained clarity.

Great job, you had an emotion!

2 Name the emotion(s) with as much specificity as possible. (Check the Emotions List)

3 Write down your emotion(s).

4 Choose one of the above emotions to start. Genuinely thank your emotion for talking to you, even if it's uncomfortable.

5 Remind yourself yo CAN resolve your emotio

6 What is the message your emotion is trying to tell you?

Why do you think your emotion is telling you this?

Where is your emotion coming from?

Physical Body

Fears

Unhelpful Thinking Style

Person

Place

Thing

Past

Is your emotion from the past? If so, you have two situations, two needs, and two resolutions. Complete the entry for the current situation and consider starting a new entry for the past situation that triggered this.

Is your emotion from an unhelpful thinking style? Study the list to see if one fits.

9 Write down what you need to do to resolve the emotion.

10 What are three things you can do today to take action to resolve the emotion?

Your emotion has helped you create a better life!

Resolving My Emotions

Emotions Action

Empowered

Examples of actions that resolve empowered.

Continue to take similar action.

Continue rehearsing thoughts that help you.

Take action based on the clarity you got.

Great job, you had an emotion!

2 Name the emotion(s) with as much specificity as possible. (Check the Emotions List)

3 Write down your emotion(s).

4 Choose one of the above emotions to start. Genuinely thank your emotion for talking to you, even if it's uncomfortable.

5 Remind yourself yo CAN resolve your emoti

6 What is the message your emotion is trying to tell you?

Why do you think your emotion is telling you this?

Where is your emotion coming from?

Physical Body

Fears

Unhelpful Thinking Style

Person

Place

Thing

Past

Is your emotion from the past? If so, you have two situations, two needs, and two resolutions. Complete the entry for the current situation and consider starting a new entry for the past situation that triggered this.

Is your emotion from an unhelpful thinking style? Study the list to see if one fits.

9 Write down what you need to do to resolve the emotion.

10 What are three things you can do today to take action to resolve the emotion?

Your emotion has helped you create a better life!

Resolving My Emotions

Emotions Messages

Sad

What could sad be telling you?

You are not getting enough care or comfort from yourself or others.

Something or someone important was lost.

Your body is not getting what it needs.

Great job, you had an emotion!

2 Name the emotion(s) with as much specificity as possible. (Check the Emotions List)

3 Write down your emotion(s).

4 Choose one of the above emotions to start. Genuinely thank your emotion for talking to you, even if it's uncomfortable.

5 Remind yourself yo CAN resolve your emotic

6 What is the message your emotion is trying to tell you?

Why do you think your emotion is telling you this?

Where is your emotion coming from?

Physical Body

Unhelpful Thinking Style

Person

Place

Thing

Past

Fears

Is your emotion from the past? If so, you have two situations, two needs, and two resolutions. Complete the entry for the current situation and consider starting a new entry for the past situation that triggered this.

Is your emotion from an unhelpful thinking style? Study the list to see if one fits.

9 Write down what you need to do to resolve the emotion.

10 What are three things you can do today to take action to resolve the emotion?

Your emotion has helped you create a better life!

Resolving My Emotions

Emotions Action

Sad

Examples of actions that resolve sadness.

Care for or comfort yourself.

Express gratitude for knowing who and what is essential in your life.

Make a plan to get enough sleep, sun, food, etc.

Great job, you had an emotion!

2 Name the emotion(s) with as much specificity as possible. (Check the Emotions List)

3 Write down your emotion(s).

4 Choose one of the above emotions to start. Genuinely thank your emotion for talking to you, even if it's uncomfortable.

5 Remind yourself y● CAN resolve your emoti●

6 What is the message your emotion is trying to tell you?

Why do you think your emotion is telling you this?

Where is your emotion coming from?

Physical Body

Fears

Unhelpful Thinking Style

Person

Place

Thing

Past

Is your emotion from the past? If so, you have two situations, two needs, and two resolutions. Complete the entry for the current situation and consider starting a new entry for the past situation that triggered this.

Is your emotion from an unhelpful thinking style? Study the list to see if one fits.

9 Write down what you need to do to resolve the emotion.

10 What are three things you can do today to take action to resolve the emotion?

Your emotion has helped you create a better life!

Resolving My Emotions

Emotions Messages

Happy

What could happy be telling you?

You are living in line with your values.

You are taking good care of yourself.

You are experiencing something meaningful to you.

Great job, you had an emotion!

2 Name the emotion(s) with as much specificity as possible. (Check the Emotions List)

3 Write down your emotion(s).

4 Choose one of the above emotions to start. Genuinely thank your emotion for talking to you, even if it's uncomfortable.

5 Remind yourself you CAN resolve your emotion

6 What is the message your emotion is trying to tell you?

Why do you think your emotion is telling you this?

Where is your emotion coming from?

Physical Body

Unhelpful Thinking Style

Fears

Person

Place

Thing

Past

Is your emotion from the past? If so, you have two situations, two needs, and two resolutions. Complete the entry for the current situation and consider starting a new entry for the past situation that triggered this.

Is your emotion from an unhelpful thinking style? Study the list to see if one fits.

9 Write down what you need to do to resolve the emotion.

10 What are three things you can do today to take action to resolve the emotion?

Your emotion has helped you create a better life!

Resolving My Emotions

Emotions Action

Happy

Examples of actions that resolve happiness.

Keep prioritizing your values.

Be intentional to keep showing yourself care.

Be mindful doing this more often.

Great job, you had an emotion!

2 Name the emotion(s) with as much specificity as possible. (Check the Emotions List)

3 Write down your emotion(s).

4 Choose one of the above emotions to start. Genuinely thank your emotion for talking to you, even if it's uncomfortable.

5 Remind yourself y̶e̶ CAN resolve your emotio̶

6 What is the message your emotion is trying to tell you?

Why do you think your emotion is telling you this?

Where is your emotion coming from?

Physical Body

Unhelpful Thinking Style

Fears

Person

Place

Thing

Past

Is your emotion from the past? If so, you have two situations, two needs, and two resolutions. Complete the entry for the current situation and consider starting a new entry for the past situation that triggered this.

Is your emotion from an unhelpful thinking style? Study the list to see if one fits.

9 Write down what you need to do to resolve the emotion.

10 What are three things you can do today to take action to resolve the emotion?

Your emotion has helped you create a better life!

Resolving My Emotions

Emotions Messages

Disgusted

What could disgusted be telling you?

> You do not like a thing, person, or topic.

> You do not value what others value.

> You are taking on the judgments of others.

Great job, you had an emotion!

2 Name the emotion(s) with as much specificity as possible. (Check the Emotions List)

3 Write down your emotion(s).

4 Choose one of the above emotions to start. Genuinely thank your emotion for talking to you, even if it's uncomfortable.

5 Remind yourself yo CAN resolve your emotio

6 What is the message your emotion is trying to tell you?

Why do you think your emotion is telling you this?

Where is your emotion coming from?

Physical Body

Unhelpful
Thinking Style

Person

Place

Thing

Past

Fears

Is your emotion from the past? If so, you have two situations, two needs, and two resolutions. Complete the entry for the current situation and consider starting a new entry for the past situation that triggered this.

Is your emotion from an unhelpful thinking style? Study the list to see if one fits.

9 Write down what you need to do to resolve the emotion.

10 What are three things you can do today to take action to resolve the emotion?

Your emotion has helped you create a better life!

Resolving My Emotions

Disgusted

Examples of actions that resolve disgust.

Avoid the thing.

Focus on living according to your values.

Let go of judgment.

Great job, you had an emotion!

2 Name the emotion(s) with as much specificity as possible. (Check the Emotions List)

3 Write down your emotion(s).

4 Choose one of the above emotions to start. Genuinely thank your emotion for talking to you, even if it's uncomfortable.

5 Remind yourself yo CAN resolve your emoti

6 What is the message your emotion is trying to tell you?

Why do you think your emotion is telling you this?

Where is your emotion coming from?

Physical Body

Fears

Unhelpful Thinking Style

Person

Place

Thing

Past

Is your emotion from the past? If so, you have two situations, two needs, and two resolutions. Complete the entry for the current situation and consider starting a new entry for the past situation that triggered this.

Is your emotion from an unhelpful thinking style? Study the list to see if one fits.

9 Write down what you need to do to resolve the emotion.

10 What are three things you can do today to take action to resolve the emotion?

Your emotion has helped you create a better life!

Resolving My Emotions

Emotions Messages

Jealous

What could jealousy be telling you?

- Someone has something you would like and can take steps to get.
- Peer pressure has defined what you value.
- You are not paying attention to what you have.

Great job, you had an emotion!

2 Name the emotion(s) with as much specificity as possible. (Check the Emotions List)

3 Write down your emotion(s).

4 Choose one of the above emotions to start. Genuinely thank your emotion for talking to you, even if it's uncomfortable.

5 Remind yourself yo CAN resolve your emotic

6 What is the message your emotion is trying to tell you?

Why do you think your emotion is telling you this?

Where is your emotion coming from?

Physical Body

Fears

Unhelpful Thinking Style

Person

Place

Thing

Past

Is your emotion from the past? If so, you have two situations, two needs, and two resolutions. Complete the entry for the current situation and consider starting a new entry for the past situation that triggered this.

Is your emotion from an unhelpful thinking style? Study the list to see if one fits.

9 Write down what you need to do to resolve the emotion.

10 What are three things you can do today to take action to resolve the emotion?

Your emotion has helped you create a better life!

Resolving My Emotions

Jealous

Examples of actions that resolve jealousy.

Outline steps to get closer to the things you want.

Focus on being your authentic self.

Pay attention to what you have.

Great job, you had an emotion!

2 Name the emotion(s) with as much specificity as possible. (Check the Emotions List)

3 Write down your emotion(s).

4 Choose one of the above emotions to start. Genuinely thank your emotion for talking to you, even if it's uncomfortable.

5 Remind yourself y[ou] CAN resolve your emoti[on]

6 What is the message your emotion is trying to tell you?

Why do you think your emotion is telling you this?

Where is your emotion coming from?

Physical Body

Fears

Unhelpful Thinking Style

Person

Place

Thing

Past

Is your emotion from the past? If so, you have two situations, two needs, and two resolutions. Complete the entry for the current situation and consider starting a new entry for the past situation that triggered this.

Is your emotion from an unhelpful thinking style? Study the list to see if one fits.

9 Write down what you need to do to resolve the emotion.

10 What are three things you can do today to take action to resolve the emotion?

Your emotion has helped you create a better life!

Resolving My Emotions

Emotions Messages

Surprised

What could surprise be telling you?

Pay close attention to something.

You are in a novel situation.

You are discovering something.

Great job, you had an emotion!

2 Name the emotion(s) with as much specificity as possible. (Check the Emotions List)

3 Write down your emotion(s).

4 Choose one of the above emotions to start. Genuinely thank your emotion for talking to you, even if it's uncomfortable.

5 Remind yourself you CAN resolve your emotic

6 What is the message your emotion is trying to tell you?

Why do you think your emotion is telling you this?

Where is your emotion coming from?

Physical Body

Fears

Unhelpful
Thinking Style

Person

Place

Thing

Past

Is your emotion from the past? If so, you have two situations, two needs, and two resolutions. Complete the entry for the current situation and consider starting a new entry for the past situation that triggered this.

Is your emotion from an unhelpful thinking style? Study the list to see if one fits.

9 Write down what you need to do to resolve the emotion.

10 What are three things you can do today to take action to resolve the emotion?

Your emotion has helped you create a better life!

Resolving My Emotions

Emotions Action

Surprised

Examples of actions that resolve surprise.

Consider if the thing is amazing or dangerous.

Assess the situation.

Incorporate the discovery into your life.

Great job, you had an emotion!

2 Name the emotion(s) with as much specificity as possible. (Check the Emotions List)

3 Write down your emotion(s).

4 Choose one of the above emotions to start. Genuinely thank your emotion for talking to you, even if it's uncomfortable.

5 Remind yourself y⬤ CAN resolve your emoti⬤

6 What is the message your emotion is trying to tell you?

Why do you think your emotion is telling you this?

Where is your emotion coming from?

Physical Body

Unhelpful Thinking Style

Person

Place

Thing

Past

Fears

Is your emotion from the past? If so, you have two situations, two needs, and two resolutions. Complete the entry for the current situation and consider starting a new entry for the past situation that triggered this.

Is your emotion from an unhelpful thinking style? Study the list to see if one fits.

9 Write down what you need to do to resolve the emotion.

10 What are three things you can do today to take action to resolve the emotion?

Your emotion has helped you create a better life!

Resolving My Emotions

Emotions Messages

Stressed

What could stress be telling you?

Something is out of alignment in your life.

You are allowing someone to pressure you.

There is something you need clarification on.

Great job, you had an emotion!

2 Name the emotion(s) with as much specificity as possible. (Check the Emotions List)

3 Write down your emotion(s).

4 Choose one of the above emotions to start. Genuinely thank your emotion for talking to you, even if it's uncomfortable.

5 Remind yourself yo CAN resolve your emotic

6 What is the message your emotion is trying to tell you?

Why do you think your emotion is telling you this?

Where is your emotion coming from?

Physical Body

Unhelpful Thinking Style

Person

Place

Thing

Past

Fears

Is your emotion from the past? If so, you have two situations, two needs, and two resolutions. Complete the entry for the current situation and consider starting a new entry for the past situation that triggered this.

Is your emotion from an unhelpful thinking style? Study the list to see if one fits.

9 Write down what you need to do to resolve the emotion.

10 What are three things you can do today to take action to resolve the emotion?

Your emotion has helped you create a better life!

Resolving My Emotions

Emotions Action

Stressed

Examples of actions that resolve stress.

Take steps to gain more alignment and balance.

Create boundaries, and say no.

Journal or ask questions to find clarity.

Great job, you had an emotion!

2 Name the emotion(s) with as much specificity as possible. (Check the Emotions List)

3 Write down your emotion(s).

4 Choose one of the above emotions to start. Genuinely thank your emotion for talking to you, even if it's uncomfortable.

5 Remind yourself y CAN resolve your emoti

6 What is the message your emotion is trying to tell you?

Why do you think your emotion is telling you this?

Where is your emotion coming from?

Physical Body

Unhelpful Thinking Style

Person

Place

Thing

Past

Fears

Is your emotion from the past? If so, you have two situations, two needs, and two resolutions. Complete the entry for the current situation and consider starting a new entry for the past situation that triggered this.

Is your emotion from an unhelpful thinking style? Study the list to see if one fits.

9 Write down what you need to do to resolve the emotion.

10 What are three things you can do today to take action to resolve the emotion?

Your emotion has helped you create a better life!

Resolving My Emotions

Emotions Messages

Fearful

What could fear be telling you?

Slow down, pay attention, and be careful.

Something reminds you of something difficult from the past.

You want to protect yourself.

Great job, you had an emotion!

2 Name the emotion(s) with as much specificity as possible. (Check the Emotions List)

3 Write down your emotion(s).

4 Choose one of the above emotions to start. Genuinely thank your emotion for talking to you, even if it's uncomfortable.

5 Remind yourself yo CAN resolve your emotio

6 What is the message your emotion is trying to tell you?

Why do you think your emotion is telling you this?

Where is your emotion coming from?

Physical Body

Fears

Unhelpful Thinking Style

Person

Place

Thing

Past

Is your emotion from the past? If so, you have two situations, two needs, and two resolutions. Complete the entry for the current situation and consider starting a new entry for the past situation that triggered this.

Is your emotion from an unhelpful thinking style? Study the list to see if one fits.

9 Write down what you need to do to resolve the emotion.

10 What are three things you can do today to take action to resolve the emotion?

Your emotion has helped you create a better life!

Resolving My Emotions

Emotions Action

Fearful

Examples of actions that resolve fear.

Offer yourself reassurance.

Resolve the past, focusing on your power and what you learned.

Take steps to protect yourself from harm.

Great job, you had an emotion!

2 Name the emotion(s) with as much specificity as possible. (Check the Emotions List)

3 Write down your emotion(s).

4 Choose one of the above emotions to start. Genuinely thank your emotion for talking to you, even if it's uncomfortable.

5 Remind yourself y⸺ CAN resolve your emoti⸺

6 What is the message your emotion is trying to tell you?

Why do you think your emotion is telling you this?

Where is your emotion coming from?

Physical Body

Unhelpful Thinking Style

Person

Place

Thing

Past

Fears

Is your emotion from the past? If so, you have two situations, two needs, and two resolutions. Complete the entry for the current situation and consider starting a new entry for the past situation that triggered this.

Is your emotion from an unhelpful thinking style? Study the list to see if one fits.

9

Write down what you need to do to resolve the emotion.

10 What are three things you can do today to take action to resolve the emotion?

Your emotion has helped you create a better life!

Resolving My Emotions

Loved

What could love be telling you?

The situation or people are safe.

You were understood by someone.

You feel valued by yourself or others.

Great job, you had an emotion!

2 Name the emotion(s) with as much specificity as possible. (Check the Emotions List)

3 Write down your emotion(s).

4 Choose one of the above emotions to start. Genuinely thank your emotion for talking to you, even if it's uncomfortable.

5 Remind yourself you CAN resolve your emotic

6 What is the message your emotion is trying to tell you?

Why do you think your emotion is telling you this?

Where is your emotion coming from?

Physical Body

Fears

Unhelpful Thinking Style

Person

Place

Thing

Past

Is your emotion from the past? If so, you have two situations, two needs, and two resolutions. Complete the entry for the current situation and consider starting a new entry for the past situation that triggered this.

Is your emotion from an unhelpful thinking style? Study the list to see if one fits.

9 Write down what you need to do to resolve the emotion.

10 What are three things you can do today to take action to resolve the emotion?

Your emotion has helped you create a better life!

Resolving My Emotions

Loved

Examples of actions that resolve loved.

Continue to spend time with people that help create this feeling.

It is safe to continue to open up.

The people around you are capable of reciprocation.

Great job, you had an emotion!

2 Name the emotion(s) with as much specificity as possible. (Check the Emotions List)

3 Write down your emotion(s).

4 Choose one of the above emotions to start. Genuinely thank your emotion for talking to you, even if it's uncomfortable.

5 Remind yourself y• CAN resolve your emoti•

6 What is the message your emotion is trying to tell you?

Why do you think your emotion is telling you this?

_____
_____
_____
_____

Where is your emotion coming from?

Physical Body

Fears

Unhelpful Thinking Style

Person

Place

Thing

Past

Is your emotion from the past? If so, you have two situations, two needs, and two resolutions. Complete the entry for the current situation and consider starting a new entry for the past situation that triggered this.

Is your emotion from an unhelpful thinking style? Study the list to see if one fits.

9 Write down what you need to do to resolve the emotion.

_____
_____
_____
_____

10 What are three things you can do today to take action to resolve the emotion?

_____
_____
_____

Your emotion has helped you create a better life!

Resolving My Emotions

Emotions Messages

Bad

What could bad be telling you?

You are making assumptions about yourself.

You realize you made a mistake.

You feel that you lack power.

Great job, you had an emotion!

2 Name the emotion(s) with as much specificity as possible. (Check the Emotions List)

3 Write down your emotion(s).

4 Choose one of the above emotions to start. Genuinely thank your emotion for talking to you, even if it's uncomfortable.

5 Remind yourself yo CAN resolve your emotic

6 What is the message your emotion is trying to tell you?

Why do you think your emotion is telling you this?

Where is your emotion coming from?

Physical Body

Unhelpful Thinking Style

Person

Place

Thing

Past

Fears

Is your emotion from the past? If so, you have two situations, two needs, and two resolutions. Complete the entry for the current situation and consider starting a new entry for the past situation that triggered this.

Is your emotion from an unhelpful thinking style? Study the list to see if one fits.

9 Write down what you need to do to resolve the emotion.

10 What are three things you can do today to take action to resolve the emotion?

Your emotion has helped you create a better life!

Resolving My Emotions

Emotions Action

Bad

Examples of actions that resolve feeling bad.

Stop making assumptions.

Apologize, and make a plan to avoid the mistake in the future.

Make a new plan based on what you learned.

Great job, you had an emotion!

2 Name the emotion(s) with as much specificity as possible. (Check the Emotions List)

3 Write down your emotion(s).

4 Choose one of the above emotions to start. Genuinely thank your emotion for talking to you, even if it's uncomfortable.

5 Remind yourself yo CAN resolve your emoti

6 What is the message your emotion is trying to tell you?

Why do you think your emotion is telling you this?

Where is your emotion coming from?

Physical Body

Unhelpful Thinking Style

Fears

Person

Place

Thing

Past

Is your emotion from the past? If so, you have two situations, two needs, and two resolutions. Complete the entry for the current situation and consider starting a new entry for the past situation that triggered this.

Is your emotion from an unhelpful thinking style? Study the list to see if one fits.

9 Write down what you need to do to resolve the emotion.

10 What are three things you can do today to take action to resolve the emotion?

Your emotion has helped you create a better life!

Resolving My Emotions

Emotions Messages

Hopeful

What could hopeful be telling you?

You envision a positive future.

Your have clarity on how to solve a problem.

You are motivated to create change.

Great job, you had an emotion!

2 Name the emotion(s) with as much specificity as possible. (Check the Emotions List)

3 Write down your emotion(s).

4 Choose one of the above emotions to start. Genuinely thank your emotion for talking to you, even if it's uncomfortable.

5 Remind yourself yo CAN resolve your emotic

6 What is the message your emotion is trying to tell you?

Why do you think your emotion is telling you this?

Where is your emotion coming from?

Physical Body

Fears

Unhelpful Thinking Style

Person

Place

Thing

Past

Is your emotion from the past? If so, you have two situations, two needs, and two resolutions. Complete the entry for the current situation and consider starting a new entry for the past situation that triggered this.

Is your emotion from an unhelpful thinking style? Study the list to see if one fits.

9 Write down what you need to do to resolve the emotion.

10 What are three things you can do today to take action to resolve the emotion?

Your emotion has helped you create a better life!

Resolving My Emotions

Emotions Action

Hopeful

Examples of actions that resolve hope.

Continue to envision a good future.

Implement problem-solving techniques.

Take steps to create change.

Great job, you had an emotion!

2 Name the emotion(s) with as much specificity as possible. (Check the Emotions List)

3 Write down your emotion(s).

4 Choose one of the above emotions to start. Genuinely thank your emotion for talking to you, even if it's uncomfortable.

5 Remind yourself yo CAN resolve your emoti

6 What is the message your emotion is trying to tell you?

Why do you think your emotion is telling you this?

Where is your emotion coming from?

Physical Body

Unhelpful Thinking Style

Person

Place

Thing

Past

Fears

Is your emotion from the past? If so, you have two situations, two needs, and two resolutions. Complete the entry for the current situation and consider starting a new entry for the past situation that triggered this.

Is your emotion from an unhelpful thinking style? Study the list to see if one fits.

9 Write down what you need to do to resolve the emotion.

10 What are three things you can do today to take action to resolve the emotion?

Your emotion has helped you create a better life!

Resolving My Emotions

Emotions Messages

Worthless

What could worthless be telling you?

You are not giving time or attention to your strengths.

You are not involved in things you value.

Someone is holding you to impossible standards.

Great job, you had an emotion!

2 Name the emotion(s) with as much specificity as possible. (Check the Emotions List)

3 Write down your emotion(s).

4 Choose one of the above emotions to start. Genuinely thank your emotion for talking to you, even if it's uncomfortable.

5 Remind yourself yo CAN resolve your emotic

6 What is the message your emotion is trying to tell you?

Why do you think your emotion is telling you this?

Where is your emotion coming from?

Physical Body

Unhelpful Thinking Style

Person

Place

Thing

Past

Fears

Is your emotion from the past? If so, you have two situations, two needs, and two resolutions. Complete the entry for the current situation and consider starting a new entry for the past situation that triggered this.

Is your emotion from an unhelpful thinking style? Study the list to see if one fits.

9 Write down what you need to do to resolve the emotion.

10 What are three things you can do today to take action to resolve the emotion?

Your emotion has helped you create a better life!

Resolving My Emotions

Worthless

Examples of actions that resolve worthless.

Ruthlessly focus on finding and building strengths.

Take values assessments or research how to find your values.

Set boundaries, and don't hold yourself to impossible standards.

Great job, you had an emotion!

2 Name the emotion(s) with as much specificity as possible. (Check the Emotions List)

3 Write down your emotion(s).

4 Choose one of the above emotions to start. Genuinely thank your emotion for talking to you, even if it's uncomfortable.

5 Remind yourself yo CAN resolve your emoti

6 What is the message your emotion is trying to tell you?

Why do you think your emotion is telling you this?

Where is your emotion coming from?

Physical Body

Fears

Unhelpful Thinking Style

Person

Place

Thing

Past

Is your emotion from the past? If so, you have two situations, two needs, and two resolutions. Complete the entry for the current situation and consider starting a new entry for the past situation that triggered this.

Is your emotion from an unhelpful thinking style? Study the list to see if one fits.

9 Write down what you need to do to resolve the emotion.

10 What are three things you can do today to take action to resolve the emotion?

Your emotion has helped you create a better life!

Resolving My Emotions

Emotions Messages

Disappointed

What could disappointed be telling you?

Your expectations were not met.

Someone you trust is not trustworthy.

You are not keeping an open mind.

Great job, you had an emotion!

2 Name the emotion(s) with as much specificity as possible. (Check the Emotions List)

3 Write down your emotion(s).

4 Choose one of the above emotions to start. Genuinely thank your emotion for talking to you, even if it's uncomfortable.

5 Remind yourself yo CAN resolve your emotio

6 What is the message your emotion is trying to tell you?

Why do you think your emotion is telling you this?

Where is your emotion coming from?

Physical Body

Fears

Unhelpful Thinking Style

Person

Place

Thing

Past

Is your emotion from the past? If so, you have two situations, two needs, and two resolutions. Complete the entry for the current situation and consider starting a new entry for the past situation that triggered this.

Is your emotion from an unhelpful thinking style? Study the list to see if one fits.

9 Write down what you need to do to resolve the emotion.

10 What are three things you can do today to take action to resolve the emotion?

Your emotion has helped you create a better life!

Resolving My Emotions

Emotions Action

Disappointed

Examples of actions that resolve disappointment.

Be mindful of holding expectations loosely.

Do not continue trusting someone who is untrustworthy.

Consider solutions to avoid disappointment in the future.

Great job, you had an emotion!

2 Name the emotion(s) with as much specificity as possible. (Check the Emotions List)

3 Write down your emotion(s).

4 Choose one of the above emotions to start. Genuinely thank your emotion for talking to you, even if it's uncomfortable.

5 Remind yourself you CAN resolve your emotion

6 What is the message your emotion is trying to tell you?

Why do you think your emotion is telling you this?

Where is your emotion coming from?

Physical Body

Fears

Unhelpful Thinking Style

Person

Place

Thing

Past

Is your emotion from the past? If so, you have two situations, two needs, and two resolutions. Complete the entry for the current situation and consider starting a new entry for the past situation that triggered this.

Is your emotion from an unhelpful thinking style? Study the list to see if one fits.

9 Write down what you need to do to resolve the emotion.

10 What are three things you can do today to take action to resolve the emotion?

Your emotion has helped you create a better life!

Resolving My Emotions

Emotions Messages

Peaceful

What could peace be telling you?

Your life has harmony and balance.

You are present at the moment.

The environment is not making many demands.

Great job, you had an emotion!

2 Name the emotion(s) with as much specificity as possible. (Check the Emotions List)

3 Write down your emotion(s).

4 Choose one of the above emotions to start. Genuinely thank your emotion for talking to you, even if it's uncomfortable.

5 Remind yourself yo CAN resolve your emotio

6 What is the message your emotion is trying to tell you?

Why do you think your emotion is telling you this?

Where is your emotion coming from?

Physical Body

Fears

Unhelpful Thinking Style

Person

Place

Thing

Past

Is your emotion from the past? If so, you have two situations, two needs, and two resolutions. Complete the entry for the current situation and consider starting a new entry for the past situation that triggered this.

Is your emotion from an unhelpful thinking style? Study the list to see if one fits.

9 Write down what you need to do to resolve the emotion.

10 What are three things you can do today to take action to resolve the emotion?

Your emotion has helped you create a better life!

Resolving My Emotions

Emotions Action

Peaceful

Examples of actions that resolve peace.

What you are doing is good for you.

Continue to practice being present.

Spend more time in these environments.

Great job, you had an emotion!

2 Name the emotion(s) with as much specificity as possible. (Check the Emotions List)

3 Write down your emotion(s).

4 Choose one of the above emotions to start. Genuinely thank your emotion for talking to you, even if it's uncomfortable.

5 Remind yourself y~~ou~~ CAN resolve your emoti~~on~~

6 What is the message your emotion is trying to tell you?

Why do you think your emotion is telling you this?

Where is your emotion coming from?

Physical Body

Unhelpful Thinking Style

Person

Place

Thing

Past

Fears

Is your emotion from the past? If so, you have two situations, two needs, and two resolutions. Complete the entry for the current situation and consider starting a new entry for the past situation that triggered this.

Is your emotion from an unhelpful thinking style? Study the list to see if one fits.

9 Write down what you need to do to resolve the emotion.

10 What are three things you can do today to take action to resolve the emotion?

Your emotion has helped you create a better life!

Resolving My Emotions

Emotions Messages

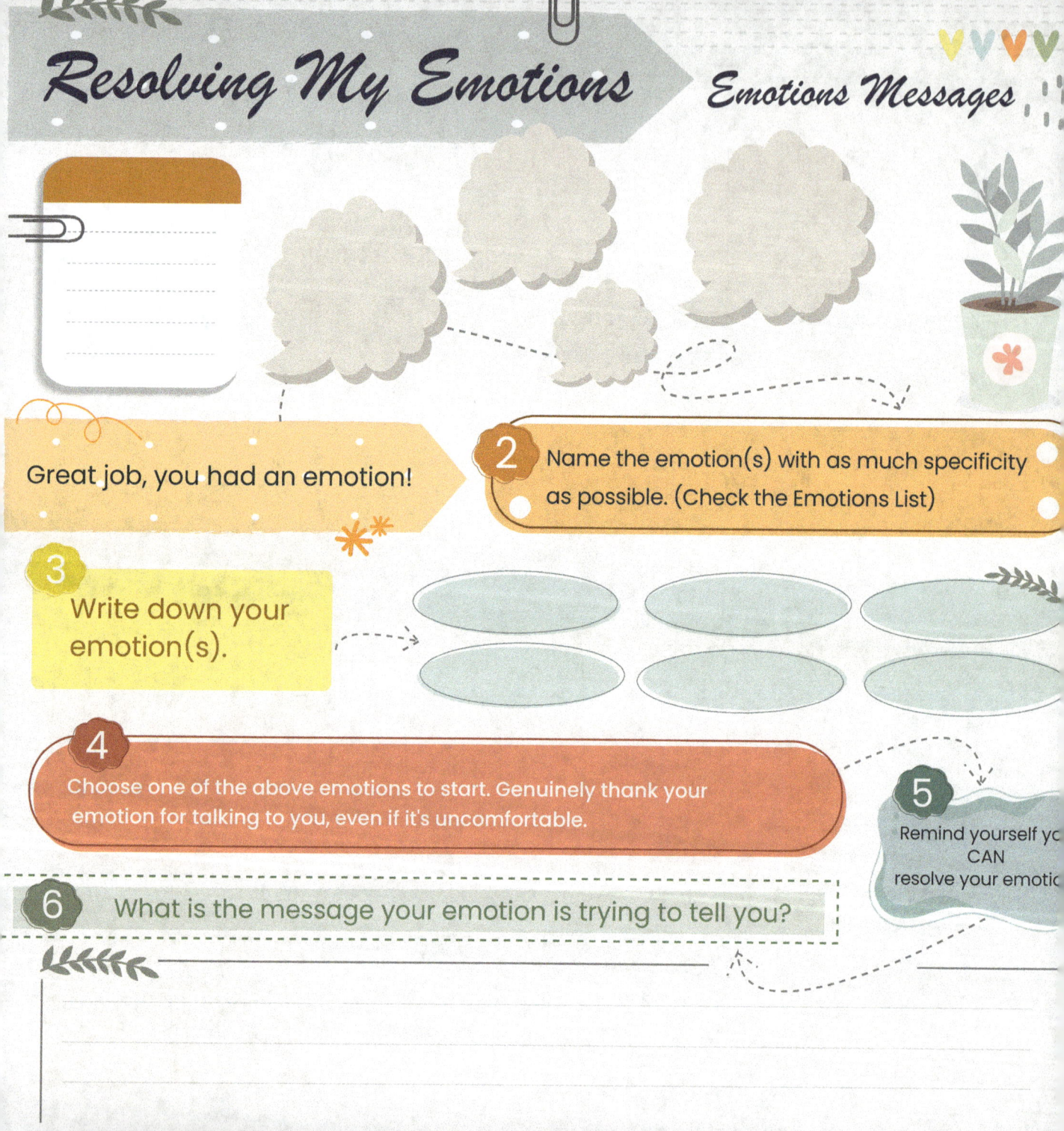

Great job, you had an emotion!

2 Name the emotion(s) with as much specificity as possible. (Check the Emotions List)

3 Write down your emotion(s).

4 Choose one of the above emotions to start. Genuinely thank your emotion for talking to you, even if it's uncomfortable.

5 Remind yourself yo CAN resolve your emotio

6 What is the message your emotion is trying to tell you?

Why do you think your emotion is telling you this?

Where is your emotion coming from?

Physical Body

Unhelpful Thinking Style

Person

Place

Thing

Past

Fears

Is your emotion from the past? If so, you have two situations, two needs, and two resolutions. Complete the entry for the current situation and consider starting a new entry for the past situation that triggered this.

Is your emotion from an unhelpful thinking style? Study the list to see if one fits.

9 Write down what you need to do to resolve the emotion.

10 What are three things you can do today to take action to resolve the emotion?

Your emotion has helped you create a better life!

Resolving My Emotions

Great job, you had an emotion!

2 Name the emotion(s) with as much specificity as possible. (Check the Emotions List)

3 Write down your emotion(s).

4 Choose one of the above emotions to start. Genuinely thank your emotion for talking to you, even if it's uncomfortable.

5 Remind yourself you CAN resolve your emoti[on]

6 What is the message your emotion is trying to tell you?

Why do you think your emotion is telling you this?

Where is your emotion coming from?

Physical Body

Fears

Unhelpful Thinking Style

Person

Place

Thing

Past

Is your emotion from the past? If so, you have two situations, two needs, and two resolutions. Complete the entry for the current situation and consider starting a new entry for the past situation that triggered this.

Is your emotion from an unhelpful thinking style? Study the list to see if one fits.

9 Write down what you need to do to resolve the emotion.

10 What are three things you can do today to take action to resolve the emotion?

Your emotion has helped you create a better life!

Resolving My Emotions

Great job, you had an emotion!

2 Name the emotion(s) with as much specificity as possible. (Check the Emotions List)

3 Write down your emotion(s).

4 Choose one of the above emotions to start. Genuinely thank your emotion for talking to you, even if it's uncomfortable.

5 Remind yourself yo CAN resolve your emotio

6 What is the message your emotion is trying to tell you?

Why do you think your emotion is telling you this?

Where is your emotion coming from?

Physical Body

Fears

Unhelpful Thinking Style

Person

Place

Thing

Past

Is your emotion from the past? If so, you have two situations, two needs, and two resolutions. Complete the entry for the current situation and consider starting a new entry for the past situation that triggered this.

Is your emotion from an unhelpful thinking style? Study the list to see if one fits.

9 Write down what you need to do to resolve the emotion.

10 What are three things you can do today to take action to resolve the emotion?

Your emotion has helped you create a better life!

Resolving My Emotions

Emotions Action

Great job, you had an emotion!

2 Name the emotion(s) with as much specificity as possible. (Check the Emotions List)

3 Write down your emotion(s).

4 Choose one of the above emotions to start. Genuinely thank your emotion for talking to you, even if it's uncomfortable.

5 Remind yourself you CAN resolve your emotion

6 What is the message your emotion is trying to tell you?

Why do you think your emotion is telling you this?

Where is your emotion coming from?

Physical Body

Fears

Unhelpful Thinking Style

Person

Place

Thing

Past

Is your emotion from the past? If so, you have two situations, two needs, and two resolutions. Complete the entry for the current situation and consider starting a new entry for the past situation that triggered this.

Is your emotion from an unhelpful thinking style? Study the list to see if one fits.

9 Write down what you need to do to resolve the emotion.

10 What are three things you can do today to take action to resolve the emotion?

Your emotion has helped you create a better life!

Resolving My Emotions

Emotions Messages

Great job, you had an emotion!

2 Name the emotion(s) with as much specificity as possible. (Check the Emotions List)

3 Write down your emotion(s).

4 Choose one of the above emotions to start. Genuinely thank your emotion for talking to you, even if it's uncomfortable.

5 Remind yourself yo CAN resolve your emotic

6 What is the message your emotion is trying to tell you?

Why do you think your emotion is telling you this?

Where is your emotion coming from?

Physical Body

Fears

Unhelpful
Thinking Style

Person

Place

Thing

Past

Is your emotion from the past? If so, you have two situations, two needs, and two resolutions. Complete the entry for the current situation and consider starting a new entry for the past situation that triggered this.

Is your emotion from an unhelpful thinking style? Study the list to see if one fits.

9 Write down what you need to do to resolve the emotion.

10 What are three things you can do today to take action to resolve the emotion?

Your emotion has helped you create a better life!

Resolving My Emotions

Great job, you had an emotion!

2 Name the emotion(s) with as much specificity as possible. (Check the Emotions List)

3 Write down your emotion(s).

4 Choose one of the above emotions to start. Genuinely thank your emotion for talking to you, even if it's uncomfortable.

5 Remind yourself y_ CAN resolve your emoti_

6 What is the message your emotion is trying to tell you?

Why do you think your emotion is telling you this?

Where is your emotion coming from?

Physical Body

Fears

Unhelpful Thinking Style

Person

Place

Thing

Past

Is your emotion from the past? If so, you have two situations, two needs, and two resolutions. Complete the entry for the current situation and consider starting a new entry for the past situation that triggered this.

Is your emotion from an unhelpful thinking style? Study the list to see if one fits.

9 Write down what you need to do to resolve the emotion.

10 What are three things you can do today to take action to resolve the emotion?

Your emotion has helped you create a better life!

Resolving My Emotions

Great job, you had an emotion!

2 Name the emotion(s) with as much specificity as possible. (Check the Emotions List)

3 Write down your emotion(s).

4 Choose one of the above emotions to start. Genuinely thank your emotion for talking to you, even if it's uncomfortable.

5 Remind yourself you CAN resolve your emotion

6 What is the message your emotion is trying to tell you?

Why do you think your emotion is telling you this?

Where is your emotion coming from?

Physical Body

Fears

Unhelpful Thinking Style

Person

Place

Thing

Past

Is your emotion from the past? If so, you have two situations, two needs, and two resolutions. Complete the entry for the current situation and consider starting a new entry for the past situation that triggered this.

Is your emotion from an unhelpful thinking style? Study the list to see if one fits.

9 Write down what you need to do to resolve the emotion.

10 What are three things you can do today to take action to resolve the emotion?

Your emotion has helped you create a better life!

Resolving My Emotions

Emotions Action

Great job, you had an emotion!

2 Name the emotion(s) with as much specificity as possible. (Check the Emotions List)

3 Write down your emotion(s).

4 Choose one of the above emotions to start. Genuinely thank your emotion for talking to you, even if it's uncomfortable.

5 Remind yourself y... CAN resolve your emoti...

6 What is the message your emotion is trying to tell you?

Why do you think your emotion is telling you this?

Where is your emotion coming from?

Physical Body

Unhelpful Thinking Style

Person

Place

Thing

Past

Fears

Is your emotion from the past? If so, you have two situations, two needs, and two resolutions. Complete the entry for the current situation and consider starting a new entry for the past situation that triggered this.

Is your emotion from an unhelpful thinking style? Study the list to see if one fits.

9 Write down what you need to do to resolve the emotion.

10 What are three things you can do today to take action to resolve the emotion?

Your emotion has helped you create a better life!

Resolving My Emotions

Emotions Messages

Great job, you had an emotion!

2 Name the emotion(s) with as much specificity as possible. (Check the Emotions List)

3 Write down your emotion(s).

4 Choose one of the above emotions to start. Genuinely thank your emotion for talking to you, even if it's uncomfortable.

5 Remind yourself you CAN resolve your emotion

6 What is the message your emotion is trying to tell you?

Why do you think your emotion is telling you this?

Where is your emotion coming from?

Physical Body

Fears

Unhelpful Thinking Style

Person

Place

Thing

Past

Is your emotion from the past? If so, you have two situations, two needs, and two resolutions. Complete the entry for the current situation and consider starting a new entry for the past situation that triggered this.

Is your emotion from an unhelpful thinking style? Study the list to see if one fits.

9 Write down what you need to do to resolve the emotion.

10 What are three things you can do today to take action to resolve the emotion?

Your emotion has helped you create a better life!

Resolving My Emotions

Great job, you had an emotion!

2 Name the emotion(s) with as much specificity as possible. (Check the Emotions List)

3 Write down your emotion(s).

4 Choose one of the above emotions to start. Genuinely thank your emotion for talking to you, even if it's uncomfortable.

5 Remind yourself y CAN resolve your emoti

6 What is the message your emotion is trying to tell you?

Why do you think your emotion is telling you this?

Where is your emotion coming from?

Physical Body

Fears

Unhelpful
Thinking Style

Person

Place

Thing

Past

Is your emotion from the past? If so, you have two situations, two needs, and two resolutions. Complete the entry for the current situation and consider starting a new entry for the past situation that triggered this.

Is your emotion from an unhelpful thinking style? Study the list to see if one fits.

9

Write down what you need to do to resolve the emotion.

10 What are three things you can do today to take action to resolve the emotion?

Your emotion has helped you create a better life!

Resolving My Emotions

Emotions Messages

Great job, you had an emotion!

2 Name the emotion(s) with as much specificity as possible. (Check the Emotions List)

3 Write down your emotion(s).

4 Choose one of the above emotions to start. Genuinely thank your emotion for talking to you, even if it's uncomfortable.

5 Remind yourself yo CAN resolve your emotic

6 What is the message your emotion is trying to tell you?

Why do you think your emotion is telling you this?

Where is your emotion coming from?

Physical Body

Fears

Unhelpful Thinking Style

Person

Place

Thing

Past

Is your emotion from the past? If so, you have two situations, two needs, and two resolutions. Complete the entry for the current situation and consider starting a new entry for the past situation that triggered this.

Is your emotion from an unhelpful thinking style? Study the list to see if one fits.

9 Write down what you need to do to resolve the emotion.

10 What are three things you can do today to take action to resolve the emotion?

Your emotion has helped you create a better life!

Resolving My Emotions

Great job, you had an emotion!

2 Name the emotion(s) with as much specificity as possible. (Check the Emotions List)

3 Write down your emotion(s).

4 Choose one of the above emotions to start. Genuinely thank your emotion for talking to you, even if it's uncomfortable.

5 Remind yourself y CAN resolve your emoti

6 What is the message your emotion is trying to tell you?

Why do you think your emotion is telling you this?

Where is your emotion coming from?

Physical Body

Unhelpful Thinking Style

Fears

Person

Place

Thing

Past

Is your emotion from the past? If so, you have two situations, two needs, and two resolutions. Complete the entry for the current situation and consider starting a new entry for the past situation that triggered this.

Is your emotion from an unhelpful thinking style? Study the list to see if one fits.

9 Write down what you need to do to resolve the emotion.

10 What are three things you can do today to take action to resolve the emotion?

Your emotion has helped you create a better life!

Resolving My Emotions

Emotions Messages

Great job, you had an emotion!

2 Name the emotion(s) with as much specificity as possible. (Check the Emotions List)

3 Write down your emotion(s).

4 Choose one of the above emotions to start. Genuinely thank your emotion for talking to you, even if it's uncomfortable.

5 Remind yourself you CAN resolve your emotion

6 What is the message your emotion is trying to tell you?

Why do you think your emotion is telling you this?

Where is your emotion coming from?

Physical Body

Unhelpful Thinking Style

Person

Place

Thing

Past

Fears

Is your emotion from the past? If so, you have two situations, two needs, and two resolutions. Complete the entry for the current situation and consider starting a new entry for the past situation that triggered this.

Is your emotion from an unhelpful thinking style? Study the list to see if one fits.

9

Write down what you need to do to resolve the emotion.

10 What are three things you can do today to take action to resolve the emotion?

Your emotion has helped you create a better life!

Resolving My Emotions

Emotions Action

Great job, you had an emotion!

2 Name the emotion(s) with as much specificity as possible. (Check the Emotions List)

3 Write down your emotion(s).

4 Choose one of the above emotions to start. Genuinely thank your emotion for talking to you, even if it's uncomfortable.

5 Remind yourself y● CAN resolve your emoti●

6 What is the message your emotion is trying to tell you?

Why do you think your emotion is telling you this?

Where is your emotion coming from?

Physical Body

Unhelpful Thinking Style

Person

Place

Thing

Past

Is your emotion from the past? If so, you have two situations, two needs, and two resolutions. Complete the entry for the current situation and consider starting a new entry for the past situation that triggered this.

Is your emotion from an unhelpful thinking style? Study the list to see if one fits.

Fears

9 Write down what you need to do to resolve the emotion.

10 What are three things you can do today to take action to resolve the emotion?

Your emotion has helped you create a better life!

Resolving My Emotions

Emotions Messages

Great job, you had an emotion!

2 Name the emotion(s) with as much specificity as possible. (Check the Emotions List)

3 Write down your emotion(s).

4 Choose one of the above emotions to start. Genuinely thank your emotion for talking to you, even if it's uncomfortable.

5 Remind yourself yo CAN resolve your emotic

6 What is the message your emotion is trying to tell you?

Why do you think your emotion is telling you this?

Where is your emotion coming from?

Physical Body

Fears

Unhelpful Thinking Style

Person

Place

Thing

Past

Is your emotion from the past? If so, you have two situations, two needs, and two resolutions. Complete the entry for the current situation and consider starting a new entry for the past situation that triggered this.

Is your emotion from an unhelpful thinking style? Study the list to see if one fits.

9 Write down what you need to do to resolve the emotion.

10 What are three things you can do today to take action to resolve the emotion?

Your emotion has helped you create a better life!

Resolving My Emotions

Emotions Action

Great job, you had an emotion!

2 Name the emotion(s) with as much specificity as possible. (Check the Emotions List)

3 Write down your emotion(s).

4 Choose one of the above emotions to start. Genuinely thank your emotion for talking to you, even if it's uncomfortable.

5 Remind yourself y___ CAN resolve your emoti___

6 What is the message your emotion is trying to tell you?

Why do you think your emotion is telling you this?

_____
_____
_____

Where is your emotion coming from?

Physical Body

Fears

Unhelpful Thinking Style

Person

Place

Thing

Past

Is your emotion from the past? If so, you have two situations, two needs, and two resolutions. Complete the entry for the current situation and consider starting a new entry for the past situation that triggered this.

Is your emotion from an unhelpful thinking style? Study the list to see if one fits.

9 Write down what you need to do to resolve the emotion.

_____
_____
_____

10 What are three things you can do today to take action to resolve the emotion?

_____
_____
_____

Your emotion has helped you create a better life!

Resolving My Emotions

Emotions Messages

Great job, you had an emotion!

2 Name the emotion(s) with as much specificity as possible. (Check the Emotions List)

3 Write down your emotion(s).

4 Choose one of the above emotions to start. Genuinely thank your emotion for talking to you, even if it's uncomfortable.

5 Remind yourself you CAN resolve your emotion

6 What is the message your emotion is trying to tell you?

Why do you think your emotion is telling you this?

Where is your emotion coming from?

Physical Body

Unhelpful
Thinking Style

Fears

Person

Place

Thing

Past

Is your emotion from the past? If so, you have two situations, two needs, and two resolutions. Complete the entry for the current situation and consider starting a new entry for the past situation that triggered this.

Is your emotion from an unhelpful thinking style? Study the list to see if one fits.

9 Write down what you need to do to resolve the emotion.

10 What are three things you can do today to take action to resolve the emotion?

Your emotion has
helped you create
a better life!

Resolving My Emotions

Emotions Action

Great job, you had an emotion!

2 Name the emotion(s) with as much specificity as possible. (Check the Emotions List)

3 Write down your emotion(s).

4 Choose one of the above emotions to start. Genuinely thank your emotion for talking to you, even if it's uncomfortable.

5 Remind yourself y CAN resolve your emoti

6 What is the message your emotion is trying to tell you?

Why do you think your emotion is telling you this?

Where is your emotion coming from?

Physical Body

Unhelpful Thinking Style

Person

Place

Thing

Past

Fears

Is your emotion from the past? If so, you have two situations, two needs, and two resolutions. Complete the entry for the current situation and consider starting a new entry for the past situation that triggered this.

Is your emotion from an unhelpful thinking style? Study the list to see if one fits.

9 Write down what you need to do to resolve the emotion.

10 What are three things you can do today to take action to resolve the emotion?

Your emotion has helped you create a better life!

Resolving My Emotions

Emotions Messages

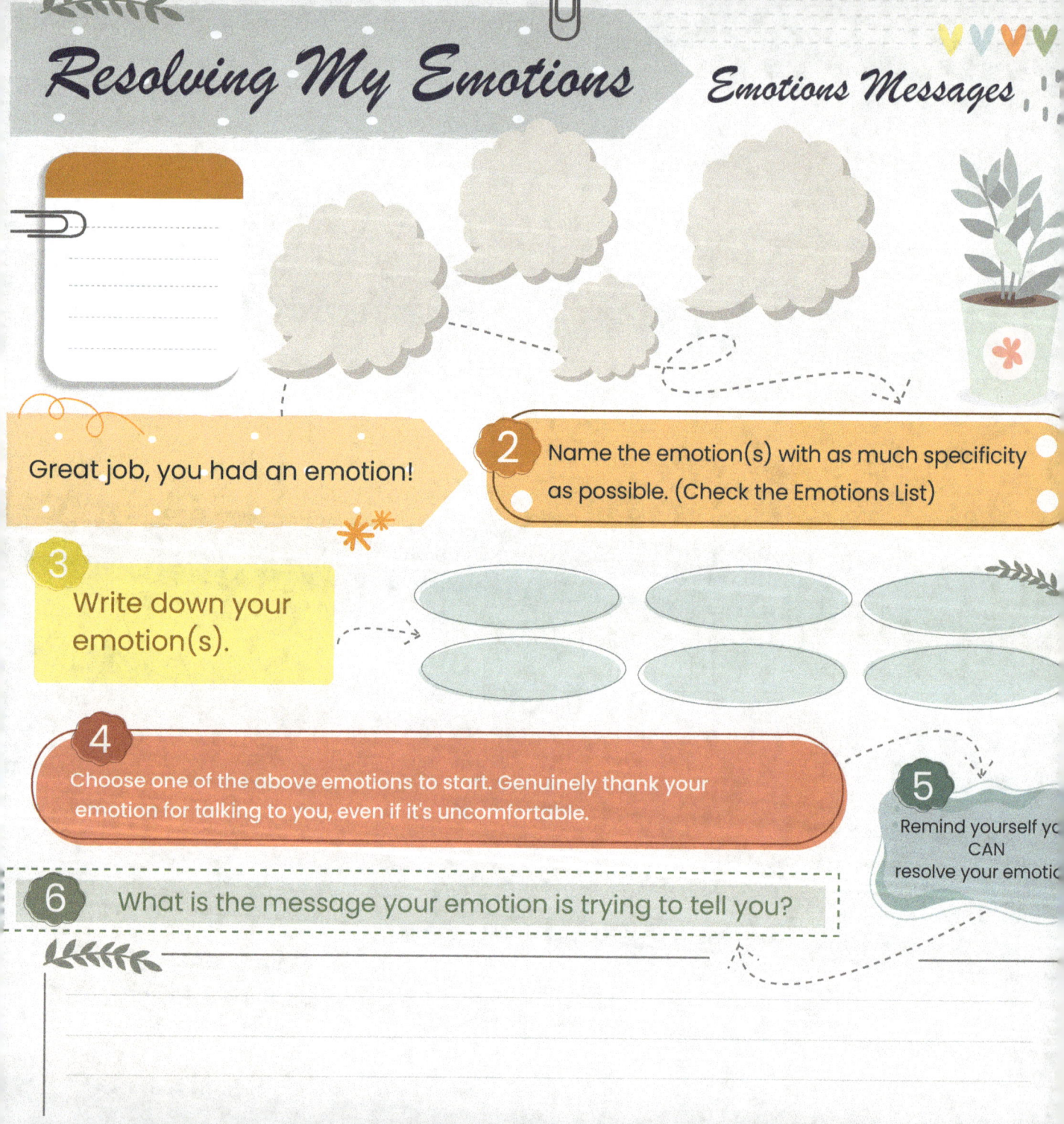

Great job, you had an emotion!

2 Name the emotion(s) with as much specificity as possible. (Check the Emotions List)

3 Write down your emotion(s).

4 Choose one of the above emotions to start. Genuinely thank your emotion for talking to you, even if it's uncomfortable.

5 Remind yourself you CAN resolve your emotion

6 What is the message your emotion is trying to tell you?

Why do you think your emotion is telling you this?

Where is your emotion coming from?

Physical Body

Fears

Unhelpful Thinking Style

Person

Place

Thing

Past

Is your emotion from the past? If so, you have two situations, two needs, and two resolutions. Complete the entry for the current situation and consider starting a new entry for the past situation that triggered this.

Is your emotion from an unhelpful thinking style? Study the list to see if one fits.

9 Write down what you need to do to resolve the emotion.

10 What are three things you can do today to take action to resolve the emotion?

Your emotion has helped you create a better life!

Resolving My Emotions

Emotions Action

Great job, you had an emotion!

2 Name the emotion(s) with as much specificity as possible. (Check the Emotions List)

3 Write down your emotion(s).

4 Choose one of the above emotions to start. Genuinely thank your emotion for talking to you, even if it's uncomfortable.

5 Remind yourself y... CAN resolve your emoti...

6 What is the message your emotion is trying to tell you?

Why do you think your emotion is telling you this?

Where is your emotion coming from?

Physical Body

Unhelpful Thinking Style

Person

Place

Thing

Past

Fears

Is your emotion from the past? If so, you have two situations, two needs, and two resolutions. Complete the entry for the current situation and consider starting a new entry for the past situation that triggered this.

Is your emotion from an unhelpful thinking style? Study the list to see if one fits.

9 Write down what you need to do to resolve the emotion.

10 What are three things you can do today to take action to resolve the emotion?

Your emotion has helped you create a better life!

Resolving My Emotions

Emotions Messages

Great job, you had an emotion!

2 Name the emotion(s) with as much specificity as possible. (Check the Emotions List)

3 Write down your emotion(s).

4 Choose one of the above emotions to start. Genuinely thank your emotion for talking to you, even if it's uncomfortable.

5 Remind yourself you CAN resolve your emotion

6 What is the message your emotion is trying to tell you?

Why do you think your emotion is telling you this?

Where is your emotion coming from?

Physical Body

Fears

Unhelpful Thinking Style

Person

Place

Thing

Past

Is your emotion from the past? If so, you have two situations, two needs, and two resolutions. Complete the entry for the current situation and consider starting a new entry for the past situation that triggered this.

Is your emotion from an unhelpful thinking style? Study the list to see if one fits.

9 Write down what you need to do to resolve the emotion.

10 What are three things you can do today to take action to resolve the emotion?

Your emotion has helped you create a better life!

Resolving My Emotions

Great job, you had an emotion!

2 Name the emotion(s) with as much specificity as possible. (Check the Emotions List)

3 Write down your emotion(s).

4 Choose one of the above emotions to start. Genuinely thank your emotion for talking to you, even if it's uncomfortable.

5 Remind yourself y CAN resolve your emoti

6 What is the message your emotion is trying to tell you?

Why do you think your emotion is telling you this?

Where is your emotion coming from?

Physical Body

Fears

Unhelpful Thinking Style

Person

Place

Thing

Past

Is your emotion from the past? If so, you have two situations, two needs, and two resolutions. Complete the entry for the current situation and consider starting a new entry for the past situation that triggered this.

Is your emotion from an unhelpful thinking style? Study the list to see if one fits.

9 Write down what you need to do to resolve the emotion.

10 What are three things you can do today to take action to resolve the emotion?

Your emotion has helped you create a better life!

Resolving My Emotions

Great job, you had an emotion!

2 Name the emotion(s) with as much specificity as possible. (Check the Emotions List)

3 Write down your emotion(s).

4 Choose one of the above emotions to start. Genuinely thank your emotion for talking to you, even if it's uncomfortable.

5 Remind yourself you CAN resolve your emotion

6 What is the message your emotion is trying to tell you?

Why do you think your emotion is telling you this?

Where is your emotion coming from?

Physical Body

Fears

Unhelpful Thinking Style

Person

Place

Thing

Past

Is your emotion from the past? If so, you have two situations, two needs, and two resolutions. Complete the entry for the current situation and consider starting a new entry for the past situation that triggered this.

Is your emotion from an unhelpful thinking style? Study the list to see if one fits.

9 Write down what you need to do to resolve the emotion.

10 What are three things you can do today to take action to resolve the emotion?

Your emotion has helped you create a better life!

Resolving My Emotions

Great job, you had an emotion!

2 Name the emotion(s) with as much specificity as possible. (Check the Emotions List)

3 Write down your emotion(s).

4 Choose one of the above emotions to start. Genuinely thank your emotion for talking to you, even if it's uncomfortable.

5 Remind yourself y
CAN
resolve your emoti

6 What is the message your emotion is trying to tell you?

Why do you think your emotion is telling you this?

Where is your emotion coming from?

Physical Body

Unhelpful Thinking Style

Person

Place

Thing

Past

Fears

Is your emotion from the past? If so, you have two situations, two needs, and two resolutions. Complete the entry for the current situation and consider starting a new entry for the past situation that triggered this.

Is your emotion from an unhelpful thinking style? Study the list to see if one fits.

9

Write down what you need to do to resolve the emotion.

10 What are three things you can do today to take action to resolve the emotion?

Your emotion has helped you create a better life!

Resolving My Emotions

Emotions Messages

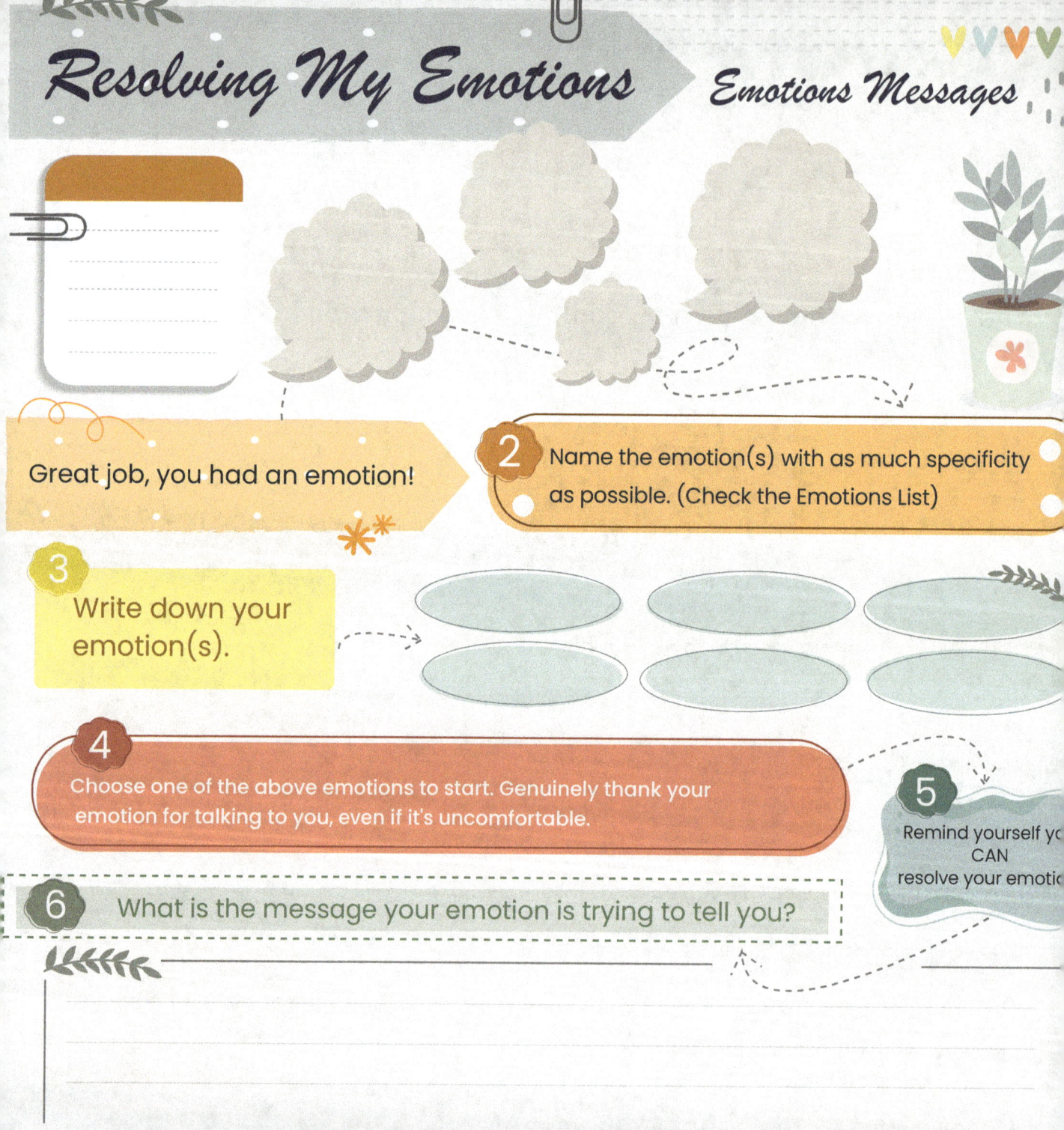

Great job, you had an emotion!

2 Name the emotion(s) with as much specificity as possible. (Check the Emotions List)

3 Write down your emotion(s).

4 Choose one of the above emotions to start. Genuinely thank your emotion for talking to you, even if it's uncomfortable.

5 Remind yourself yc CAN resolve your emotic

6 What is the message your emotion is trying to tell you?

Why do you think your emotion is telling you this?

Where is your emotion coming from?

Physical Body

Fears

Unhelpful Thinking Style

Person

Place

Thing

Past

Is your emotion from the past? If so, you have two situations, two needs, and two resolutions. Complete the entry for the current situation and consider starting a new entry for the past situation that triggered this.

Is your emotion from an unhelpful thinking style? Study the list to see if one fits.

9 Write down what you need to do to resolve the emotion.

10 What are three things you can do today to take action to resolve the emotion?

Your emotion has helped you create a better life!

Resolving My Emotions

Emotions Action

Great job, you had an emotion!

2 Name the emotion(s) with as much specificity as possible. (Check the Emotions List)

3 Write down your emotion(s).

4 Choose one of the above emotions to start. Genuinely thank your emotion for talking to you, even if it's uncomfortable.

5 Remind yourself y
CAN
resolve your emoti

6 What is the message your emotion is trying to tell you?

Why do you think your emotion is telling you this?

Where is your emotion coming from?

Physical Body

Unhelpful Thinking Style

Person

Place

Thing

Past

Fears

Is your emotion from the past? If so, you have two situations, two needs, and two resolutions. Complete the entry for the current situation and consider starting a new entry for the past situation that triggered this.

Is your emotion from an unhelpful thinking style? Study the list to see if one fits.

9 Write down what you need to do to resolve the emotion.

10 What are three things you can do today to take action to resolve the emotion?

Your emotion has helped you create a better life!

Resolving My Emotions

Emotions Messages

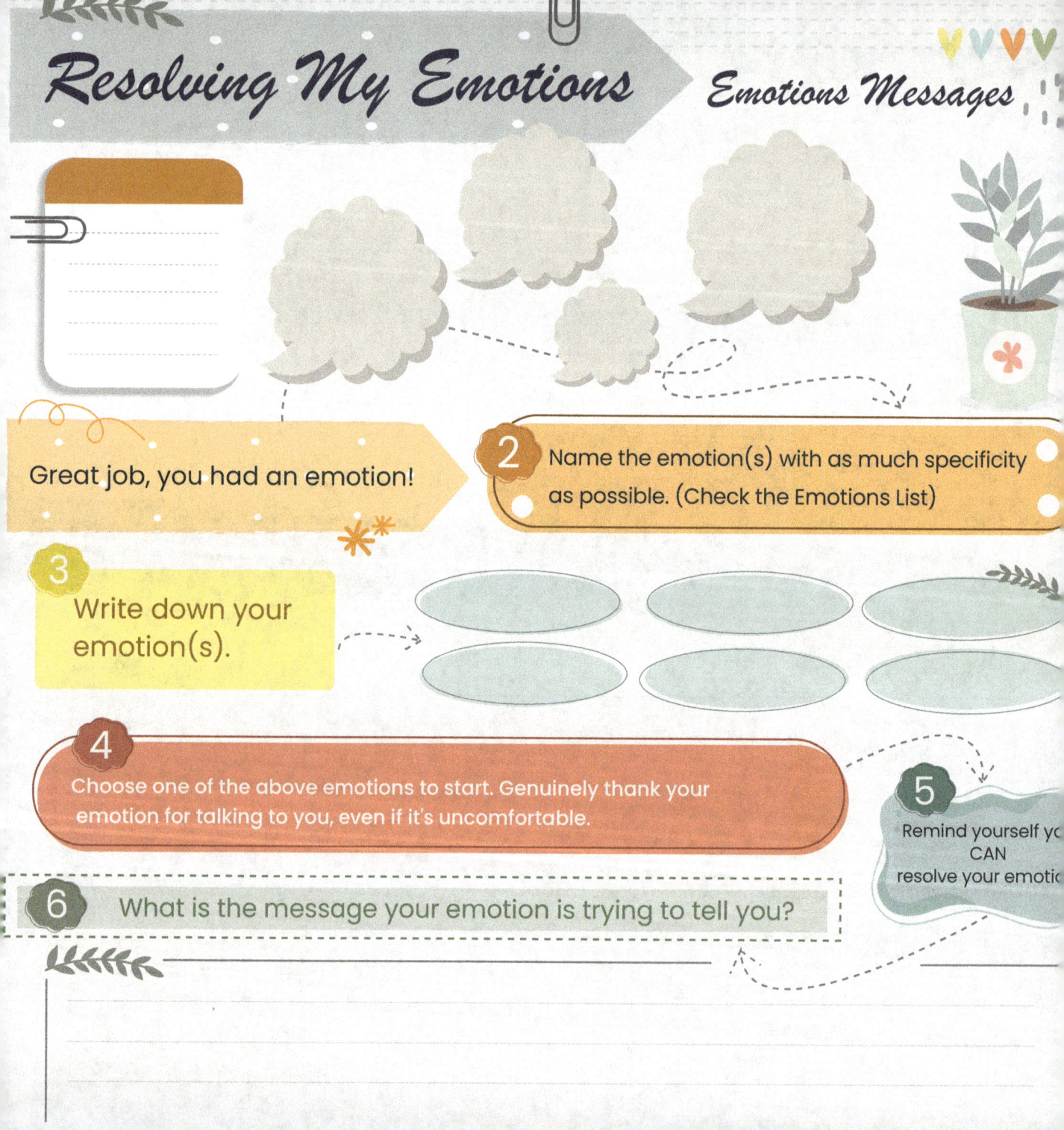

Great job, you had an emotion!

2 Name the emotion(s) with as much specificity as possible. (Check the Emotions List)

3 Write down your emotion(s).

4 Choose one of the above emotions to start. Genuinely thank your emotion for talking to you, even if it's uncomfortable.

5 Remind yourself yo CAN resolve your emotio

6 What is the message your emotion is trying to tell you?

Why do you think your emotion is telling you this?

Where is your emotion coming from?

Physical Body

Fears

Unhelpful Thinking Style

Person

Place

Thing

Past

Is your emotion from the past? If so, you have two situations, two needs, and two resolutions. Complete the entry for the current situation and consider starting a new entry for the past situation that triggered this.

Is your emotion from an unhelpful thinking style? Study the list to see if one fits.

9 Write down what you need to do to resolve the emotion.

10 What are three things you can do today to take action to resolve the emotion?

Your emotion has helped you create a better life!

Resolving My Emotions

Emotions Action

Great job, you had an emotion!

2 Name the emotion(s) with as much specificity as possible. (Check the Emotions List)

3 Write down your emotion(s).

4 Choose one of the above emotions to start. Genuinely thank your emotion for talking to you, even if it's uncomfortable.

5 Remind yourself y CAN resolve your emoti

6 What is the message your emotion is trying to tell you?

Why do you think your emotion is telling you this?

Where is your emotion coming from?

Physical Body

Fears

Unhelpful Thinking Style

Person

Place

Thing

Past

Is your emotion from the past? If so, you have two situations, two needs, and two resolutions. Complete the entry for the current situation and consider starting a new entry for the past situation that triggered this.

Is your emotion from an unhelpful thinking style? Study the list to see if one fits.

9 Write down what you need to do to resolve the emotion.

10 What are three things you can do today to take action to resolve the emotion?

Your emotion has helped you create a better life!

Resolving My Emotions

Emotions Messages

Great job, you had an emotion!

2 Name the emotion(s) with as much specificity as possible. (Check the Emotions List)

3 Write down your emotion(s).

4 Choose one of the above emotions to start. Genuinely thank your emotion for talking to you, even if it's uncomfortable.

5 Remind yourself yo CAN resolve your emotic

6 What is the message your emotion is trying to tell you?

Why do you think your emotion is telling you this?

Where is your emotion coming from?

Physical Body

Fears

Unhelpful Thinking Style

Person

Place

Thing

Past

Is your emotion from the past? If so, you have two situations, two needs, and two resolutions. Complete the entry for the current situation and consider starting a new entry for the past situation that triggered this.

Is your emotion from an unhelpful thinking style? Study the list to see if one fits.

9

Write down what you need to do to resolve the emotion.

10 What are three things you can do today to take action to resolve the emotion?

Your emotion has helped you create a better life!

Resolving My Emotions

Great job, you had an emotion!

2 Name the emotion(s) with as much specificity as possible. (Check the Emotions List)

3 Write down your emotion(s).

4 Choose one of the above emotions to start. Genuinely thank your emotion for talking to you, even if it's uncomfortable.

5 Remind yourself y___ CAN resolve your emoti___

6 What is the message your emotion is trying to tell you?

Why do you think your emotion is telling you this?

Where is your emotion coming from?

Physical Body

Unhelpful
Thinking Style

Person

Place

Thing

Past

Fears

Is your emotion from the past? If so, you have two situations, two needs, and two resolutions. Complete the entry for the current situation and consider starting a new entry for the past situation that triggered this.

Is your emotion from an unhelpful thinking style? Study the list to see if one fits.

9 Write down what you need to do to resolve the emotion.

10 What are three things you can do today to take action to resolve the emotion?

Your emotion has helped you create a better life!

Emotions and Feelings Glossary

Acceptance	the action of consenting to receive or undertake something offered
Admiration	respect and warm approval
Adoration	deep love and respect
Affection	a gentle feeling of fondness or liking
Afraid	feeling fear or anxiety; frightened
Agitation	a state of anxiety or nervous excitement
Agony	extreme physical or mental suffering
Aggressive	ready or likely to attack or confront
Alarm	an anxious awareness of danger
Alarmed	frightened or concerned that one may be in danger or that something undesirable will happen
Alienation	the state or experience of being isolated from a group or an activity to which one should belong or in which one should be involved
Amazement	a feeling of great surprise or wonder
Ambivalence	the state of having mixed feelings or contradictory ideas about something or someone
Amusement	the state or experience of finding something funny
Anger	a strong feeling of annoyance, displeasure, or hostility
Anguish	severe mental or physical pain or suffering
Annoyed	slightly angry; irritated
Anticipating	regard as probable; expect or predict
Anxious	experiencing worry, unease, or nervousness, typically about an imminent event or something with an uncertain outcome
Apathy	lack of interest, enthusiasm, or concern
Apprehension	anxiety or fear that something bad or unpleasant will happen
Arrogant	having or revealing an exaggerated sense of one's own importance or abilities
Assertive	having or showing a confident and forceful personality
Astonished	greatly surprised or impressed; amazed
Attentiveness	the action of paying close attention to something
Attraction	the action or power of evoking interest, pleasure, or liking for someone or something
Aversion	a strong dislike or disinclination
Awe	a feeling of reverential respect mixed with fear or wonder
Baffled	totally bewilder or perplex

Bewildered	perplexed and confused, very puzzled
Bitter	having a sharp, pungent taste or smell; not sweet
Bliss	perfect happiness; great joy
Bored	feeling weary because one is unoccupied or lacks interest in one's current activity
Brooding	showing deep unhappiness of thought.
Calm	not showing or feeling nervousness, anger, or other strong emotions
Carefree	free from anxiety or responsibility.
Careless	not giving sufficient attention or thought to avoid harm or errors.
Caring	displaying kindness and concern for others
Charity	an organization set up to provide help and raise money for those in need.
Cheeky	impudent or irreverent, typically in an endearing or amusing way
Cheerfulness	the quality or state of being noticeably happy and optimistic
Claustrophobic	(of a person) having an extreme or irrational fear of confined places
Coercive	relating to or using force or threats
Comfortable	(especially with clothes or furnishings), providing physical ease and relaxation.
Confident	feeling or showing confidence in oneself; self-assured
Confusion	lack of understanding; uncertainty
Contempt	the feeling that a person or a thing is beneath consideration, worthless, or deserving of scorn
Content	in a state of peaceful happiness
Courage	the ability to do something that frightens one
Cowardly	lacking courage
Cruelty	callous indifference to or pleasure in causing pain and suffering
Curiosity	a strong desire to know or learn something
Cynicism	an inclination to believe that people are motivated purely by self-interest; skepticism
Dazed	unable to think or react properly; bewildered
Dejection	a sad and depressed state; low spirits
Delighted	feeling or showing great pleasure
Demoralized	having lost confidence or hope; disheartened
Depressed	(of a person) in a state of general unhappiness or despondency
Desire	a strong feeling of wanting to have something or wishing for something to happen
Despair	the complete loss or absence of hope
Determined	having made a firm decision and being resolved not to change it
Disappointment	sadness or displeasure caused by the nonfulfillment of one's hopes or expectations

Disbelief	inability or refusal to accept that something is true or real
Discombobulated	confused and disconcerted.
Discomfort	slight pain
Discontentment	lack of contentment; dissatisfaction with one's circumstances
Disgruntled	angry or dissatisfied
Disgust	a feeling of revulsion or strong disapproval aroused by something unpleasant or offensive
Disheartened	having lost determination or confidence; dispirited
Dislike	feeling distaste for or hostility toward
Dismay	consternation and distress, typically caused by something unexpected
Disoriented	having lost one's sense of direction
Dispirited	having lost enthusiasm and hope; disheartened
Displeasure	a feeling of annoyance or disapproval
Distraction	a thing that prevents someone from giving full attention to something else
Distress	extreme anxiety, sorrow, or pain
Disturbed	having had its normal pattern or function disrupted
Dominant	most important, powerful, or influential
Doubt	a feeling of uncertainty or lack of conviction
Dread	anticipate with great apprehension or fear.
Dumbstruck	so shocked or surprised as to be unable to speak
Eagerness	enthusiasm to do or to have something; keenness
Ecstasy	an overwhelming feeling of great happiness or joyful excitement
Elation	great happiness and exhilaration
Embarrassment	a feeling of self-consciousness, shame, or awkwardness
Empathy	the ability to understand and share the feelings of another
Enchanted	placed under a spell; bewitched
Enjoyment	the state or process of taking pleasure in something
Enlightened	having or showing a rational, modern, and well-informed outlook
Ennui	a feeling of listlessness and dissatisfaction arising from a lack of occupation or excitement
Enthusiasm	intense and eager enjoyment, interest, or approval
Envy	a feeling of discontented or resentful longing aroused by someone else's possessions, qualities, or luck
Euphoria	a feeling or state of intense excitement and happiness
Exasperated	intensely irritated and frustrated
Excitement	a feeling of great enthusiasm and eagerness
Expectancy	the state of thinking or hoping that something, especially something pleasant, will happen or be the case
Fascination	the power to fascinate someone; the quality of being fascinating

Fear	an unpleasant emotion caused by the belief that someone or something is dangerous, likely to cause pain or a threat
Flakey	breaking or separating easily into small, thin pieces
Focused	able to see clearly
Fondness	affection or liking for someone or something
Friendliness	the quality of being friendly; affability
Fright	a sudden, intense feeling of fear
Frustrated	feeling or expressing distress and annoyance, especially because of the inability to change or achieve something
Fury	wild or violent anger
Glee	a great delight
Gloomy	dark or poorly lit, especially so as to appear depressing or frightening
Gratitude	the quality of being thankful; readiness to show appreciation for and to return kindness
Greed	the intense and selfish desire for something, especially wealth, power, or food
Grief	deep sorrow, especially that caused by someone's death
Grouch	a habitually grumpy person
Grumpy	bad-tempered and irritable
Guilty	culpable of or responsible for a specified wrongdoing
Happiness	the state of being happy
Hatred	feel intense or passionate dislike
Helpless	unable to defend oneself or to act without help
Homesickness	a feeling of longing for one's home during a period of absence from it
Hope	a feeling of expectation and desire for a certain thing to happen.
Hopeless	feeling or causing despair about something
Horrified	filled with horror; extremely shocked
Hospitable	friendly and welcoming to strangers or guests
Humiliation	the action of humiliating someone or the state of being humiliated
Humility	a modest or low view of one's own importance; humbleness
Hurt	cause physical pain or injury to
Hysteria	exaggerated or uncontrollable emotion or excitement
Idleness	laziness; indolence
Impatient	having or showing a tendency to be quickly irritated or provoked
Indifference	lack of interest, concern, or sympathy
Indignant	feeling or showing anger or annoyance at what is perceived as unfair treatment
Infatuation	an intense but short-lived passion or admiration for someone or something

Infuriated	make (someone) extremely angry and impatient.
Insecurity	uncertainty or anxiety about oneself; lack of confidence
Insightful	having or showing an accurate and deep understanding; perceptive
Insulted	speaking to or treating with disrespect or scornful abuse
Interest	the state of wanting to know or learn about something or someone
Intrigued	arouse the curiosity or interest of; fascinate
Irritated	showing or feeling slight anger; annoyed
Isolated	far away from other places, buildings, or people; remote
Jealousy	the state or feeling of being jealous
Jovial	cheerful and friendly
Joy	a feeling of great pleasure and happiness
Jubilation	a feeling of great happiness and triumph
Kind	a group of people or things having similar characteristics
Lazy	unwilling to work or use energy
Liking	a feeling of regard or fondness.
Loathing	a feeling of intense dislike or disgust; hatred.
Lonely	sad because one has no friends or company.
Longing	a yearning desire
Loopy	crazy or silly.
Love	an intense feeling of deep affection
Lust	very strong sexual desire
Mad	very angry
Melancholy	a feeling of pensive sadness, typically with no obvious cause.
Miserable	wretchedly unhappy or uncomfortable
Miserliness	the excessive desire to save money; extreme meanness
Mixed up	suffering from psychological or emotional problems
Modesty	the quality or state of being unassuming or moderate in the estimation of one's abilities
Moody	given to unpredictable changes of mood, especially sudden bouts of gloominess or sullenness
Mortified	cause (someone) to feel embarrassed, ashamed, or humiliated
Mystified	utterly bewildered or perplex
Nasty	highly unpleasant, especially to the senses; physically nauseating
Nauseated	make (someone) feel sick; affect with nausea
Negative	not desirable or optimistic
Neglect	fail to care for properly.
Nervous	easily agitated or alarmed
Nostalgic	characterized by or exhibiting feelings of nostalgia
Numb	deprived of the power of sensation

Obstinate	stubbornly refusing to change one's opinion or chosen course of action despite attempts to persuade one to do so
Offended	resentful or annoyed, typically as a result of a perceived insult
Optimistic	hopeful and confident about the future
Outrage	an extremely strong reaction of anger, shock, or indignation
Overwhelmed	drowned beneath a huge mass
Panicked	feel or cause to feel panic
Paranoid	unreasonably or obsessively anxious, suspicious, or mistrustful
Passion	strong and barely controllable emotion
Patience	the capacity to accept or tolerate delay, trouble, or suffering without getting angry or upset
Pensiveness	engaged in, involving, or reflecting deep or serious thought
Perplexed	completely baffled; very puzzled
Persevering	continuing in a course of action despite difficulty or delay in achieving success
Pessimism	a tendency to see the worst aspect of things or believe that the worst will happen; a lack of hope or confidence in the future
Pity	the feeling of sorrow and compassion caused by the suffering and misfortunes of others.
Pleased	feeling or showing pleasure and satisfaction, especially at an event or a situation
Pleasure	a feeling of happiness satisfaction, and enjoyment
Politeness	behavior that is respectful and considerate of other people
Positive	constructive, optimistic, or confident
Possessive	demanding someone's total attention and love
Powerless	without ability, influence, or power.
Pride	a feeling of deep pleasure or satisfaction derived from one's own achievements, the achievements of those with whom one is closely associated, or from qualities or possessions that are widely admired
Puzzled	unable to understand; perplexed
Rage	violent, uncontrollable anger
Rash	displaying or proceeding from a lack of careful consideration of the possible consequences of an action
Rattled	make or cause to make a rapid succession of short, sharp knocking sounds, typically as a result of shaking and striking repeatedly against a hard surface or object
Regret	feel sad, repentant, or disappointed over (something that has happened or been done, especially a loss or missed opportunity)
Rejected	dismiss as inadequate, inappropriate, or not to one's taste

Relaxed	free from tension and anxiety; at ease
Relieved	no longer feeling distressed or anxious; reassured
Reluctant	unwilling and hesitant; disinclined
Remorse	deep regret or guilt for a wrong committed
Resentment	bitter indignation at having been treated unfairly
Resignation	an act of retiring or giving up a position
Restlessness	the inability to rest or relax as a result of anxiety or boredom
Revulsion	a sense of disgust and loathing
Ruthless	having or showing no pity or compassion for others
Sadness	the condition or quality of being sad
Satisfaction	fulfillment of one's wishes, expectations, or needs, or the pleasure derived from this
Scared	fearful; frightened
Schadenfreude	pleasure derived by someone from another person's misfortune
Scorn	the feeling or belief that someone or something is worthless or despicable; contempt
Sentimentality	excessive tenderness, sadness, or nostalgia
Serenity	the state of being calm, peaceful, and untroubled
Shame	a painful feeling of humiliation or distress caused by the consciousness of wrong or foolish behavior
Shameless	(of a person or their conduct) characterized by or showing a lack of shame
Shocked	surprised and upset
Smug	having or showing an excessive pride in oneself or one's achievements
Sorrow	a feeling of deep distress caused by loss, disappointment, or other misfortune suffered by oneself or others
Spite	a desire to hurt, annoy, or offend someone
Stressed	experiencing mental or emotional strain or tension
Strong	able to withstand great force or pressure
Stubborn	having or showing dogged determination not to change one's attitude or position on something, especially in spite of good arguments or reasons to do so
Stuck	push a sharp or pointed object into or through (something)
Submissive	ready to conform to the authority or will of others; meekly obedient or passive
Suffering	the state of undergoing pain, distress, or hardship
Surprise	an unexpected or astonishing event, fact, or thing
Suspense	a state or feeling of excited or anxious uncertainty about what may happen

Emotions And Feelings Glossary

Suspicious	having or showing a cautious distrust of someone or something
Sympathy	feelings of pity and sorrow for someone else's misfortune
Tenderness	gentleness and kindness
Tension	the state of being stretched tight.
Terror	extreme fear
Thankful	pleased and relieved
Thrilled	feeling or showing great excitement and pleasure; very excited
Tired	in need of sleep or rest; weary
Tolerance	the ability or willingness to tolerate something, in particular, the existence of opinions or behavior that one does not necessarily agree with
Torment	severe physical or mental suffering
Triumphant	having won a battle or contest; victorious
Troubled	beset by problems or conflict
Trust	firm belief in the reliability, truth, ability, or strength of someone or something
Uncertainty	the state of being uncertain
Undermined	erode the base or foundation
Uneasiness	a feeling of anxiety or discomfort
Unhappy	not happy
Unnerved	make (someone) lose courage or confidence
Unsettled	lacking stability
Unsure	not feeling, showing, or doing with confidence and certainty.
Upset	make (someone) unhappy, disappointed, or worried
Vengeful	seeking to harm someone in return for a perceived injury
Vicious	deliberately cruel or violent
Vigilance	the action or state of keeping careful watch for possible danger or difficulties
Vulnerable	susceptible to physical or emotional attack or harm
Weak	lacking the power to perform physically demanding tasks; lacking physical strength and energy
Woe	great sorrow or distress (often used hyperbolically)
Worried	anxious or troubled about actual or potential problems
Worthy	having or showing the qualities or abilities that merit recognition in a specified way
Wrath	extreme anger

www.ingramcontent.com/pod-product-compliance
Lightning Source LLC
Chambersburg PA
CBHW081330120626
46546CB00011B/3292